AN ANVIL ORIGINAL
Under the general editorship of Louis L. Snyder

NATIONALISM AND REALISM: 1852–1879

Volume II of A HISTORY OF THE EUROPEAN CENTURY 1814-1917

HANS KOHN
Professor Emeritus of History
The City University of New York

D. VAN NOSTRAND COMPANY, INC.
PRINCETON, NEW JERSEY
TORONTO · MELBOURNE · LONDON

To Prof. Felix E. Hirsch
in friendship

———————————————————

VAN NOSTRAND REGIONAL OFFICES
New York, Chicago, San Francisco

D. VAN NOSTRAND COMPANY, LTD., *London*
D. VAN NOSTRAND COMPANY (Canada), LTD., *Toronto*
D. VAN NOSTRAND COMPANY PTY. LTD., *Melbourne*

COPYRIGHT, 1968, BY
HANS KOHN
Published simultaneously in Canada by
D. VAN NOSTRAND COMPANY (Canada), LTD.

PRINTED IN THE UNITED STATES OF AMERICA

Preface

This is the second volume of *A History of the European Century 1814-1917,* a continuation of *Absolutism and Democracy 1814-1852.* That first period of the nineteenth century was in many ways a prolongation of the eighteenth century. Life in Europe was, as regards society and social structure, technology, and communications, not fundamentally different from the preceding age. European society was mostly rural and status-bound. Between 1852 and 1879 a profound change occurred: industrialization penetrated into France and Central Europe; communications and the pace of life quickened; the commercial and professional middle classes on the European continent grew in numbers and influence. But they no longer opposed, together with artisans and workers, the long established authorities of monarchy and aristocracy. Frightened by the new problems of an industrial society, they entered into an alliance with the old ruling classes who on their part accepted the trends of constitutionalism and nationalism—which in the preceding period had been staunchly resisted by Metternich and propagated by the middle classes, in alliance with the artisans and workers of the larger cities, against the monarchy, the aristocracy, and the church.

This new alignment of forces changed the character of nationalism from the populist "idealism" of a Mazzini, Michelet, Lamennais or Garibaldi, to the "realism" of a Bismarck or Cavour. The emphasis shifted from the "people" to "power," from "liberty" to "order," from the optimistic belief in the natural goodness of man, peoples, and history either to the pessimistic over-evaluation of the authority of the state or to the faith in the supra-individual and positivist guidance by science. From 1815 to 1852 international peace prevailed on the whole in Europe, and the armaments race was no burden on the na-

tions of the continent; from 1852 to 1879 national wars of
unification or independence—principally in Italy, Germany, and
the Balkans—accelerated the armaments race and narrowed the
limits set by the new nation-states upon the liberty of the individual. The wars—including the War between the States in
North America—speeded the development of technology and
promoted the growth of a martial spirit. The chief exception to
this trend was Britain under the leadership of Gladstone. There
the introduction of compulsory military service and the growing
influence of the military establishment remained unknown. Britain
also stayed outside the system of military alliances, the beginning
of which on the European continent coincided with the end of
the period discussed in this volume. These pacts set the pattern
for the tensions which led to the Great War of 1914. Thus the
final breakdown of the relatively peaceful European system
which had been established in 1815 was prepared during the
three decades from 1852 to 1879.

This book again presents in its second part—as all Anvil
Books do—some of the characteristic and often-difficult-to-ob-
tain original sources of the period. It was written in the course
of the year which I spent in Philadelphia as a professor of history
at Saint Joseph's College. To that institution my gratitude is
due for its friendly hospitality.

HANS KOHN

Table of Contents

Part I

NATIONALISM AND REALISM

CHAPTER 1

Changes in European Life and Thought

The Acceleration of Communication. During the three decades from 1850 to 1880 the process of industrialization and urbanization which earlier had transformed Britain into the "workshop of the world" reached the European continent. France under Napoleon III and Germany after the victory over France in 1870 entered into competition with Britain. The old rural European society with the leisurely pace of life and its slight social and geographic mobility, which still existed in 1840, gave way to a new, more dynamic and more complex way of life. The improvement of the food supply and the advances in medical knowledge put an end to the formerly almost stagnant size of population. In the course of the nineteenth century the population of Europe more than doubled: estimated at 188 millions in 1800, it grew to 266 millions by 1850 and to 400 millions in 1900. Agriculture improved by the application of science and technology, especially the use of chemical fertilizers. Justus Liebig (1803-1873), a German chemist who helped the development of artificial fertilizers, published in 1840 his *Organic Chemistry in its Applications to Agriculture and Physiology*. Cyrus McCormick (1809-1884), the son of an American blacksmith, started the first mass production of agricultural machinery in the United States, and a similar development set in with the introduction of the Croskill reaper in Britain. In the following decades agriculture became less of a drudgery in the advanced countries; at the same time many rural workers migrated into cities and provided there the manpower for industrialization. The three decades ended the period of recurrent famines in western Europe.

The growing density of population coincided with and made possible the use and acceleration of new means of transportation and communication, which started to break down the age-old isolation of villages and thereby allowed the formation of modern nations. In the 1840's railroads began to be built on a rapidly

growing scale, and the mail service was extended to ever widen-
ing circles of population. The Northern military leaders in the
War between the States in North America and the Prussian general staff pioneered in the 1860's in the strategic use of railroads, which in these wars for national unity became at the
same time instruments of national unification. More rapid transportation, cheaper and uniform postage rates, the growing literacy
of the population increased the amount of mail many times and
led in 1875 to the establishment of the Universal Postal Union
with its seat in Berne, Switzerland. Its chief promoter was Heinrich von Stephan (1831-1897), the first "minister of post" of the
new German Empire.

The next important step in the acceleration of communication
was taken by a patent granted in 1848 in the United States to
Samuel Morse (1791-1872) for his magnetic telegraph. By 1861
Morse patents were working in Europe, and in 1865 the first
submarine cable was laid to connect England with America. In
the same year Napoleon III called an international conference to
Paris where twenty states founded the International Union for
Telegraphy. It had its seat in Berne until 1948 when it was transferred to Geneva. It was then renamed the International Union
of Telecommunication and counted, in 1965, 124 member-states.

The introduction of the telegraphic transmission of speech, the
telephone, came in the last years of the three decades. The telephone was invented in Boston in 1876 by Alexander Graham
Bell (1847-1922), a Scot immigrant who had come to the United
States in 1871. The first telephonic switchboard for commercial
services was operated in New Haven, Connecticut, in 1878 with
twenty-one subscribers; the following year the first exchange was
opened in London. Thus in the period from 1850 to 1880 the
foundations were laid for the rapid acceleration of communications which was later to transform the twentieth-century world.
In the European countries post, telegraph and telephone were
nationalized, and though railroads were mainly started by private
enterprise, their chief lines were taken over by the respective
governments in the course of the century following 1850.

The Changing Mood of Europe.   The debacle of the revolutions of 1848/49, the reassertion of the traditional power of
monarchy, and the growing influence of the military establish-

ment in most continental countries put an end to the optimistic
"idealism" of the 1830's and 1840's. The influence of Hegel
waned and was replaced by that of another German, Arthur
Schopenhauer (1788-1860), a pessimist who regarded reason as
a mere instrument of the Will, which he interpreted as a blind
and impelling force, manifest in individual life and in history.
To Schopenhauer history appeared not as a road to "salvation,"
but as an endless and meaningless struggle for the self-assertion
of individuals and groups. Given the everlasting competitive conflicts with their inevitable frustrations, Schopenhauer, denying the
role of reason in history and the rationality and goodness of man,
called upon the power of the state to maintain order. But he did
not sanctify the state. Fundamentally it was to him as meaningless as all history. Ultimately the Buddhist striving for Nirvana,
for overcoming one's desires, and for renouncing all willful ambitions offered an escape from everlasting misery. Within human
existence only art, above all music, can according to Schopenhauer afford at least temporary relief through man's absorption
in a disinterested world of ideas, which for the moment stills
the driving force of Will. In 1854 the great German composer,
Richard Wagner (1813-1883), sent the text of his chief work
"The Ring of the Nibelungen" with a feeling of gratitude and
an appreciative dedication to Schopenhauer. In this monumental
cycle of four evening-filling musical tragedies, the all-pervading
lust for gold and power ends in the annihilation of the gods and
their order ("The Twilight of the Gods") and in the triumph
of primeval chaos.

Positivism. As far as optimism continued, it was generally
no longer based on a supranatural religion or on a metaphysical
faith, but on the belief in positivist science, on observation, ex-
perimentation, and verification. In 1852 Auguste Comte (1798-
1857) published his *Catechism of Positivist Religion: Summary
and Exposition of the Universal Religion*. He maintained that
mankind was entering the final stage of its history, a stage devoid
of any theological or metaphysical speculation when the "servants
of humanity"—both scientists and practical men—would direct
mankind's progress in an orderly and peaceful fashion to social
regeneration and harmony. A new note was sounded by Comte:
"The intellectual discipline instituted by Positivist Philosophy

rests on logical and scientific foundations of the utmost solidity; but no solidity can secure its prevalence, so antipathetic is its severe regime to minds trained at present, unless it can gain the support of women and the proletarian class." With theology, Comte believed, the warlike spirit would wane too. Like Kant, Comte opposed not only wars but also colonialism, as an example of which he cited the French invasion of Algeria. "I venture, in the name of true Positivists, solemnly to proclaim my wish that the Arabs may forcibly expel the French, unless the French consent to an act of noble restitution." With the decline of theology and war, "the relative will finally take the place of the absolute; altruism will tend to control egoism; systematic progress [planning] will replace spontaneous growth. Humanity will definitely occupy the place of God, but she will not forget the services which the idea of God provisionally rendered."

Comte was the first to introduce sociology as a new branch of scientific exploration. One of the most influential English thinkers of the Victorian age, Herbert Spencer (1820-1903), helped to popularize the new approach. He was not only influenced by Comte but also by Darwin. He applied the principles of evolutionary progress, the adaptation of the organism to environmental changes, as well to society as to biology and psychology. The first volume of his *The Principles of Sociology* appeared in 1876. He viewed the future with optimism: "There is warrant for the belief, that Evolution can end only in the establishment of the greatest perfection and the most complete happiness." But other and much more pessimistic conclusions could be drawn, and were drawn, from Darwinism.

Darwinism. Comte and Spencer were agnostics who rejected all theological or metaphysical speculation. Charles Darwin (1809-1882) was educated for the ministry and remained a theist after he turned to the natural sciences. His *The Origin of Species by Means of Natural Selection or the Preservation of Favored Races in the Struggle for Life* (1859) was one of the books the main thesis of which altered the currents of human thought. (*See Reading No. 1.*) Before Darwin the general public and most scientists accepted the story told in Genesis that species were immutable, created by God at the time when He created the universe. Darwin's theories gained acceptance only after years of struggle. Yet Darwin remained unshaken. The concluding sentences of his book confirm his trust in the Creator and his optimism about nature's laws: "We may look with some confidence to a secure future of great length. And as natural selection works solely by and for the good of each being, all corporal and mental endowments will tend to progress towards perfection. . . . From the war of nature, from famine and death, the most exalted object which we are capable of conceiving, namely, the production of the higher animals, directly follows. There is grandeur in this view of life, with its several powers, having been originally breathed by the Creator into a few forms or into one; and that, whilst this planet has gone cycling on according to the fixed law of gravity, from so simple a beginning endless forms most beautiful and most wonderful have been and are being evolved." Twelve years later Darwin published his book about the evolution of the most beautiful and wonderful of these forms, *The Descent of Man* (1871).

Darwinism confirmed the validity of laws in nature beyond the mathematical laws governing astronomy and physics, which were the great discovery of the seventeenth century. No longer was man a being created separately from all other creatures. He, too, became subject to nature's laws. By his integration into the great natural process he was in no way degraded, as Darwin's opponents feared. Darwin himself wrote that "science and her methods gave me a resting place independent of authority and tradition." Darwin's most active disciple, Thomas Huxley (1825-1895), an English biologist, wrote in his *Essays* that "the conception of the constancy of the order of nature has become the dominant idea of modern thought. Whatever may be man's speculative doctrines, it is quite certain that every intelligent person guides his life and risks his fortune upon the belief that the order of nature is constant, and that the chain of natural causation is never broken." The belief in progress through science diminished the belief in miracles and in the haunting ghost stories which ceased to prevail even among the masses in Western Europe. What the German social scientist Max Weber (1864-1920) called *Entzauberung*—the end of the belief in the power of magic and preternatural forces in life and nature—became characteristic of the last decades of the nineteenth century.

Darwinism exercised its influence far beyond biology. It accustomed the public to slogans like "struggle for life," "survival of the fittest," and "favored races." These concepts were transferred from the realm of evolution in nature to the willfulness of human aspirations and actions. The image of Nature changed from eighteenth-century benevolence to "red in tooth and claw" (Alfred Tennyson, 1809-1892). Struggle was accepted as an inevitable element in interpersonal and international relations; success was seen as a confirmation of the legitimacy of deeds and plans. This "social Darwinism," rejected by Darwin and Huxley, was used in the later part of the century to justify the imposition of the strong upon the weak and to disregard moral laws which apparently conflicted with the alleged "iron laws" of nature. This attitude was not new; new was only its "scientific" justification.

Industrial Technology. The growing competitive dynamism of life in the second half of the nineteenth century was not only stimulated by Darwinism but also by the general and growing systematic application of science to technology. This process has been called the "second" industrial revolution. The first had been overwhelmingly the work of practical inventors and technicians; its basis was supplied by coal and iron. After 1850 science influenced, to a rapidly growing degree, technological advance; its basis became electricity and steel. An English engineer, Sir Henry Bessemer (1813-1893), began in 1859 to manufacture in his Sheffield works steel from cast iron with the help of a new process which he invented. Ernst Werner von Siemens (1816-1892), a German industrialist, and his younger brother, Sir William Siemens (1823-1883) who emigrated to England, pioneered in electrical engineering as well as in steel production. The inventions of the German scientist Robert Bunsen (1811-1899) made the use of gas for lamps and stoves easier. The second third of the nineteenth century became the period of extensive use of gas light, not only in streets—a use known before —but also in homes, where it replaced the candle and the kerosene lamp. Soon, however, the gas burner was to be replaced by the electric bulb.

CHAPTER 2

Religious and Social Tensions

Faith, Science, and Morality. Evolution which, incompatible with the origins of man as told in Genesis, established him as part of nature, and the Higher (literary and historical as distinct from textual) Criticism of the Bible which aroused doubts regarding the divine inspiration of scripture, created serious problems for many believers. Not only generations but families were often split by these conflicts of conscience. Of the two younger brothers of Cardinal John Henry Newman (1801-1890) who was ordained in the Church of England in 1824 and was received into the Roman Church in 1845, Charles Robert was a professed atheist, and the youngest Francis William (1805-1897), professor of Latin in University College and equally proficient in mathematics and Oriental languages, was an agnostic and a member of the Unitarian Association. Agnosticism maintains that "a First Cause and an unseen world are subjects of which we know nothing." Theology lost around the middle of the century its rank as the foremost branch of scholarship. In Britain a National Secular Society was founded in 1866 by Charles Bradlaugh (1833-1891). Elected a member of the House of Commons for Northampton in 1880, he could take his seat only in 1886 because he refused to take a religious oath.

The Victorian middle class, different from that of the Continent, persevered in its strict bigotry. Yet, again different from the Continent, Evangelicalism with its concern for social justice and the common man was strong in Britain's upper classes, both among dissenting Protestants and in the Church of England. A growing number of Europeans revolted against the traditional forms of religion. Samuel Butler (1835-1902), the son of an Anglican minister and grandson of a bishop, published in 1873 *The Fair Heaven,* an ironic defense of Christian evidences. His autobiographical, satirical novel *The Way of All Flesh* was written in the 1870's but published only after his death, in 1903. He attacked the hypocrisy of the "respectable" people who

15

"would be equally horrified to hear the Christian religion doubted or to see it practiced."

Most agnostics of the period continued to identify the moral law with the traditional Christian ethics and wished to preserve its validity without a divine sanction or the dread of the day of judgment. Frederic William Henry Myers (1843-1901) recalled hearing the novelist George Eliot (Mary Ann Evans, 1819-1880)—the translator of two of the most influential German secularizing treatises, David Friedrich Strauss's *The Life of Jesus Critically Examined* and Ludwig Feuerbach's *The Essence of Christianity*—discuss during a walk on the grounds of Trinity College, Cambridge, the three words "which have been used so often as the inspired trumpet calls of men—the words God, Immortality, Duty—how inconceivable was the first, how unbelievable was the second, and yet how peremptory and absolute the third." Of Thomas Hill Green (1836-1882), professor of philosophy in Oxford, whose ethical philosophy was based on human self-determination, it was said that "a long intellectual travail had convinced him that the miraculous Christian story was untenable; speculatively he gave it up with grief and difficulty, but practically to his last hour he clung to all the forms and associations of the old belief with a wonderful affection." *

Undogmatic Ethics. The effort to salvage Christian ethics without the faith in Christian dogmas was frequently discussed in the literature of the period. The English novelist Mrs. Humphry Ward (1851-1920) dealt with it in her widely read *Robert Elsmere* (1888), in which the Oxford educated young vicar, shaken in his faith, resigned his living, not to enjoy the world but to overwork himself in the slums of London's East End and to prepare the "New Brotherhood of Christ." † The Norwegian dramatist Henrik Ibsen (1828-1906) was fascinated in his *Emperor and Galilean* (1873) by the Roman Emperor

---

* Janet Penrose Trevelyan (daughter of Mrs. Humphry Ward), *The Life of Mrs. Humphry Ward* (London, 1923), p. 63.

† The two historical English universities were secularized only after 1852. All fellows had to take Holy Orders in the Church of England until 1854, and all non-Anglican Protestants, Catholics, and Jews were excluded until 1871 by the requirement of subscribing to the thirty-nine articles of the Church of England (1563).

Julian who died in 363 at the age of thirty-two after having rejected Christianity as the final answer to man's spiritual needs. Ibsen interpreted him as seeking a synthesis of Christian ethics with pagan sensual joy of life. Ibsen later transferred this quest and its problems to a modern setting. In his play *Rosmersholm* (1886) Johannes Rosmer, the descendant of generations of conservative clergymen and formerly a clergyman himself, learns that moral nobility kills the joy of living. The absence of a Supreme Judge does not make life easier but more exacting. Being thrown upon one's individual conscience does not result in absolution and does not invite license; it imposes a more severe judgment. The rejection of traditional religion, even the unmasking of its pretensions,† did in the 1870's not imply a violation of moral standards. Only in the twentieth century under the influence of Nietzsche, Freud, D. H. Lawrence whose teachings, however, were often misinterpreted, the ethical rigorism of the leading agnostics of the nineteenth century gave way to the liberty of a supposedly life-enhancing vitality.

Anti-Clericalism on the Continent. Religious life in Britain, as was political life, was imbued on the whole with a spirit of tolerance and latitude. Such was not the case in continental Europe. There, especially in the Roman-Catholic and Greek-Orthodox countries, the clash between the traditionalism of the churches and the new scientific outlook became one of the great issues of the period. Often even natural scientists assumed the defense of traditional religion against the new claims of science. In Austria, at the celebration of the five hundredth anniversary of the University of Vienna (1865), the then Rector Joseph Hyrtl (1810-1894), a world famous authority on anatomy, extolled the superiority of the (Catholic) religion over science. On the other hand, some German Protestant writers, differing therein from Darwin, made of evolution and materialism an all-inclusive world-view (*Weltanschauung*). They regarded mind a function of matter, reducible to physical laws, as were light, heat, or

---

† In his *Ghosts* (1881) Ibsen showed "what pestilent and lethal vapours could mount from a scrupulously observed Christian marriage, from family piety and from charitable organizations." Brian W. Downs, *Ibsen* (Cambridge University Press, 1946), p. 171.

sound. All were declared subject to the "universality of determinism and of the causal relationship." This materialism rejected the belief in a personal God, in spiritual autonomy, in the freedom of will. The materialist philosophy was not new. It can be found among ancient Hindus and Greeks, and its leading eighteenth-century representative was Baron Paul Holbach (1723-1789) whose *Système de la Nature* (1770) revealed in its subtitle *"ou des lois du monde physique et du monde moral,"* that his system of nature claimed to be equally applicable to the physical as to the moral and political world.

But only in the 1860's did the materialist philosophy become widely accepted, above all among the educated Russian youth. The influence of Hegel was replaced by that of the German physician Ludwig Büchner (1824-1899) and his book *Energy and Matter* (1855). This "scientific materialism" which Friedrich Engels, the collaborator of Karl Marx, called "vulgar materialism" was also propagated by the German naturalist Karl Vogt (1817-1895), who after 1849 lived in Switzerland, and by the Dutch physiologist Jacob Moleschott (1822-1893) who taught in Italy. Materialism strengthened the anti-clericalism, the opposition to the dominant influence of the Church in political and educational life. The far-reaching claims of the Church as superior to the State and its rejection of all modern democracy contributed to the growth of anti-clericalism. In the leading democracy of Europe, in Switzerland, the federal constitution of 1848 made the establishment of the Jesuit order in Switzerland illegal. Articles 51 and 52 of the revised constitution of 1874 went even further; they permitted the suppression of other religious orders, "the action of which is dangerous for the state or disturbs the peace among the religions" and prohibited the establishment of new monasteries or religious orders.

The First Vatican Council. The anti-clerical attitude was strengthened by the then dominant trend in the Roman Church. When, after the defeat of Mazzini's Roman Republic Pope Pius IX (see *Absolutism and Democracy, 1814-1852,* pp. 96 and 103) returned to Rome, he was determined to make the Church the bulwark against all democratic and liberal ideas. The bull *Ineffabilis Deus* (December 8, 1854) proclaimed the dogma of the immaculate conception of the Virgin Mary, the first new dogma

since the Council of Trent. Ten years later followed the ency-
clical *Quanta cura* with the *Syllabus errorum,* which ruled that
the Pontiff neither can nor ought to be reconciled with progress,
liberalism, and modern civilization, with all the errors of "our
very sad age." Freedom of conscience and of thought, the rights
of man and religious liberty could not be tolerated, for in view
of the fact that the Roman Church represented the only and
unique truth, they meant freedom of self-destruction. The claims
of science were equally included in the long list of uncomprom-
ising condemnations.

Shortly thereafter preparation began for the convocation of a
Council of the Church, the first since the Council of Trent
(1545-1563) which established the militant Church of the Coun-
ter Reformation. The new Council was held in 1869/1870 at the
Vatican and went beyond the Council of Trent in accepting the
dogma of Papal infallibility. It strengthened the Pope's absolute
authority over councils and bishops and exalted the papacy over
all governments and its decisions over all science. Amid the
changing world of modern thought, the Church stood as the
immutable rock of the ages, in a voluntary seclusion from its
time, enhancing its absolutism and its centralized authority. The
new dogma aroused widespread apprehension that Catholics
might put their allegiance to the Court of Rome above the loyalty to their nation. Though these fears proved unfounded, they
strengthened anti-clericalism in countries like France and Austria (which annulled the concordat of 1855) and led to the
Kulturkampf in Bismarkian Prussia.

One day after the acceptance of the dogma of papal infallibility in St. Peter's Cathedral (July 18, 1870), the war between
France and Germany broke out. As a result of the French defeat (Napoleon III's army had protected the Papal State, now
confined to Latium, against the new Kingdom of Italy), the
millenary secular power of the Pope came to an end. Italian
troops occupied Rome on September 20, 1870, and twelve days
later a plebiscite decided for Rome becoming a part of Italy
and its capital. The Pope rejected the advances of the Italian
government, excommunicated its members, and regarded himself as a "prisoner in the Vatican." The hostility between the
Church and the Italian State ended only in 1929 with the Pact

of the Lateran, which recognized the Catholic Church as the official state-church.

Social Dissent. In spite of the spread of industrialization in France and central Europe, the organization of the new working class made little progress between 1852 and 1879. The defeat of the Parisian workers in June 1848 and the ineffectualness of the Chartists in England (see *Absolutism and Democracy, 1814-1852,* pp. 55, 99) sapped the vitality of the proletariat. The influence of Marxism grew only very slowly. In Germany the first General German Workers' Association was organized in 1863 by Ferdinand Lassalle (1825-1864), a brilliant orator. He was not an internationalist but a German patriot. After having met Bismarck, then Prussia's Prime Minister, in May 1863, he wrote him on June 8: "You will realize . . . how true it is that the working class inclines intimately toward dictatorship, once they can be convinced that the dictatorship is being exercised in their interest. They would be much inclined, as I suggested to you recently, despite their republican leanings—or rather just because of them—to accept the Crown as the natural instrument of a social dictatorship rather than the egoism of the bourgeois class; if the Crown could make up its mind to take the truly improbable step of adopting a really revolutionary national policy and turn from a monarchy of the privileged classes to a socialist people's monarchy."

In England the opposition to the existing economic order was expressed by Christian Socialists. Among their leaders were two ministers of the Church of England, John Frederick Denison Maurice (1805-1872), who became the first principal of the Working Man's College (1854) and Charles Kingsley (1819-1875), who preached a sermon on "The Message of the Church to Working Men" and whose novel "Alton Locke" (1849) showed sympathy with the Chartist leaders. The organ of the movement, *The Christian Socialist,* wrote: "A new idea has gone abroad into the world, that Socialism, the latest-born of the forces now at work in modern society, and Christianity, the eldest born of these forces, are in their nature not hostile, but akin to each other, or rather that the one is but the development, the outgrowth, the manifestation of the other, so that even the strangest and the most monstrous forms of Socialism are at bottom but Christian heresies."

The First International. Marx helped found in London in 1864 the International Working Men's Association, later known as the First International. It was neither a powerful organization nor Marxist in its outlook. The first Marxist party was launched only in 1869 in Germany by August Bebel (1840-1913) and Wilhelm Liebknecht (1826-1900) and merged in 1875 with the Association founded by Lassalle into the German Social Democratic Party. The backbone of the First International were the non-political British trade unions. Marx's leadership and his principle of a centralized state-communism was challenged by Mikhail Bakunin (1814-1876), a Russian nobleman turned revolutionary. His rejection of disciplined mass-organizations in favor of free productive associations gained many followers in Spain, in Italy, and in the French-speaking parts of Switzerland. Superior as a tactician, Marx succeeded in 1872, at the Congress of the International at The Hague, in expelling Bakunin and the anarchists. But this victory meant also the end of the International. After the grim suppression of the Paris Commune (May 1871), the general climate in Europe was highly unfavorable to any socialist activity. Thus the Congress in The Hague decided to transfer the General Council of the International to the United States where, after a shadowy existence of four years, it was dissolved at a meeting in Philadelphia. Marx set his hopes primarily in the highly-trained German industrial workers, Bakunin in the Russian peasants and in less developed countries. Events before 1914 seemed to bear out Marx's expectations. (*See Reading No. 27.*)

CHAPTER 3

Wars and Reforms, 1852-1861

The three decades from 1815 to 1848 were a period of international peace, of low armaments, of little change in the state-system established in Vienna in 1815. The following three decades from 1852 to 1879 were filled with civil and international wars and the technical improvement of armaments. The state system of 1815 underwent a fundamental change at the expense of the Habsburg and Ottoman monarchies and of France. Britain continued, unchallenged, as the greatest sea-power, and an aggrandized Prussia emerged, called the (Second) German *Reich,* as the hegemonial power on the European Continent. The period marked the end of the Holy Alliance and the loss of Habsburg leadership in Germany and in Italy. The wars of the period, however, were short wars (therein different from the American War between the States), wars of national liberation and unification, fulfilling the vague and generous aspirations of the generations of 1813 and 1848 in a far less generous way with the help of the sword and the cunning of international diplomacy. That was the case not only in central Europe, but also in the Balkans where the "Eastern Question" (see *Absolutism and Democracy, 1815-1852,* ch. 7) was being solved by the Christian Balkan peoples at the expense of Islam.

The Crimean War. The first of the series of wars, which ended with the Russian-Turkish War of 1877/78, originated in 1853 with a Russian attempt to protect the rights and privileges of the Orthodox Christian communities in Turkey. Russia occupied the two Rumanian principalities—Moldavia and Wallachia—which were Turkish protectorates, inhabited by an Orthodox population speaking a language derived from Latin. After the Russian Black Sea fleet annihilated a Turkish fleet in the port of Sinope in eastern Anatolia (November 1853), France and Britain came to Turkey's help. Britain acted as the protector of the Straits of Constantinople from Russian control, and Napoleon III wished to undo the treaties of 1815, a result of his

22

uncle's defeat, and to establish France as the protector of the Catholics in the Ottoman Empire. Later the two Western powers were joined by the kingdom of Sardinia, whose prime minister Count Camille Cavour was determined to bring up the "Italian Question" at the forthcoming peace conference. In the eyes of the Russian nationalists, the "West" came to the help of "infidel" Turkey out of a deep-seated animosity against Russia and her desire to "liberate" the Christian Balkan peoples from Turkish rule.

Austria and Russia. Austria neither joined the Western allies nor did it support Russia. Francis Joseph's vacillating attitude endeared him to neither side. The Austrians mobilized part of their army to protect the mouth of the Danube. The Russian Emperor regarded this attitude as an act of ingratitude, for he had helped the Austrians to put down the Hungarian rebellion in 1849. The future Austro-Russian divergence in their Balkan policy was foreshadowed in the tensions of the Crimean War. On the other hand, Prussia under King Frederick William IV refused to antagonize Russia, and the relations between the courts of St. Petersburg and Berlin remained cordial.

The Course of the War. The war itself brought little fame to the belligerents. It revealed the general backwardness of the absolutist regime in Russia and the military unpreparedness of the Western powers. The correspondent of *The* (London) *Times,* William Howard Russell (1821-1907), disclosed the incompetence of the British leadership. When the British commander-in-chief Field Marshal Lord Raglan (1788-1855) charged him with giving aid and comfort to the enemy, *The Times* declared in a memorable editorial that in free countries it was "the first duty of the Press to maintain the earliest and most correct intelligence of the events of the time, and instantly, by disclosing them, to make them the common property of the nation. The statesman collects his information secretly and by secret means: he keeps back the current intelligence of the day with ludicrous precautions. . . . The Press lives by disclosures."

The main battleground was the Crimean peninsula in the northern Black Sea. The British soldiers suffered more from disease than from the enemy. Florence Nightingale (1820-1910) arranged for a new systematic care for the sick and wounded.

In the military activities the fortified port of Sevastopol resisted the siege by the Western allies for a long time. (*See Reading No. 24.*) The Russian novelist Count Leo Tolstoy (1828-1910), then an officer in the Russian army, described the struggle in his stories *Sevastopol* (1855). After the fall of the fortress in September 1855, peace negotiations started in Paris. The peace congress of Paris in 1856 marked the height of Napoleon's career. He presided at the congress, which admitted Turkey as a member of the "concert of Europe." The powers promised to respect Turkish independence and territorial integrity and the Turkish Sultan promised to improve the conditions of his subjects without regard of race or creed. Both promises were not kept. Russia lost the right of sending its Black Sea fleet into the Mediterranean and the control of the mouth of the Danube. The Treaty of Paris marked also a progress in international law, especially with regard to the freedom of the seas and the security of merchandise from seizure in wartime, except for contraband of war. The Danube became an "international" waterway, open to the navigation of all nations. An international commission was established for its supervision. The Black Sea ports were opened to merchant ships of all nations in time of peace, but the Straits of Constantinople were closed to all foreign warships when Turkey was at peace.

Consequences of the Crimean War. The Crimean War put an end to the temper of the period of the Holy Alliance. Nationalism, before 1850 a revolutionary force of the Left, regarded as subversive by the governments of the Metternich period, had proclaimed the fraternity of the peoples against the absolutist regimes. It now became a Rightist movement taken over by the governments, and it carried out its goals of national independence and unity by armed force and authoritarian leadership. The faith of the pre-1848 generation in the natural goodness of the "People" and its will to international harmonious co-operation disappeared. Europe entered a period of armaments and nationalist conflicts. The new emphasis on "realism" (*Realpolitik*) and power (*Machtpolitik*) was most successfully represented by Prussia under Otto von Bismarck (1815-1898). The nobility and the upper middle class feared the workers. They looked to the monarchy as a bulwark of social order.

Austria lost the leadership on the European continent, which she had exercised from 1815 to 1852. Her conservative policy had to yield to the revolutions from above, carried through in the other countries. As a result of the wars of 1859 and 1866, Austria lost her traditional dominant position in Germany and Italy. In consequence, she turned her territorial ambitions to the Balkans where they clashed not only with Russian but also with Italian aspirations. The period which started with the Crimean War and the Congress of Paris ended with the Russian-Turkish War of 1877/8 and the Congress of Berlin. In fact, the new configuration influenced European diplomacy to the very eve of the war of 1914, the Balkan wars, and the assassination of the Habsburg Archduke Francis Ferdinand. But the most immediate effect of the Crimean War made itself felt in Russia.

Reform Movements in Russia. Nicholas I, the arch-conservative policeman of European "order," died in 1855, a few months before the end of the war. His son, Alexander II (b. 1818) liberated on March 3, 1861, the peasants from their degrading status of serfs. (*See Reading No. 2.*) Whereas the slaves in the United States received at the time of their liberation no property, the Russian serfs acquired part of the land, which they had cultivated. But the legislation was so complex that it satisfied neither the landlords nor the peasants; while the landlord economy continued to stagnate, the peasants complained of the excessive compensation which they had to pay over almost half a century. Nor did the peasants achieve real individual freedom or equality of status. Their property remained on a communal basis with yearly redistribution of the land to the members of the commune (*mir*) and, among other restrictions, they were still subject to corporal punishment.

Nevertheless, the old patriarchal order which concentrated all power in rural Russia in the hands of the nobility came to an end. This change necessitated far-reaching reforms of the judicial and administrative organs; but political freedom was not introduced, and Russia's fundamental problems remained unsolved. The imperial bureaucracy kept even the accepted reforms, especially the local self-government (*zemstvo*), within the narrowest limits possible. Yet the immobility of Russian society was broken. Many of the former serfs migrated to the cities, attracted by the opportunities of the advancing industrialization; and Alexandrinian Russia witnessed a flowering of Russian cultural life, especially in the novels and in music.

The Revolutionary Movement in Russia. The Alexandrinian reforms aroused great hopes without fulfilling them. The new generation of the Russian educated youth demanded more. Its inspiration came in the 1850's from Alexander Herzen (1812-1870) who left Russia in 1847 and ten years later started to publish in London the first free Russian newspaper *The Bell* (*Kolokol*). It was smuggled into Russia and widely read there. But in the 1860's Herzen's liberalism did no longer satisfy the young generation. Ivan Turgenev (1818-1883) presented in his novel *Fathers and Children* (1861) their representative in Bazarov, a medical student dedicated to science and to an active life in the service of a future better society. The radical youth turned away from the esthetic and contemplative idealism of its fathers. Its spokesman became the critic and economist Nicholas Chernyshevski (1828-1889), who asked the question *What is to be done?* and tried to answer it in form of a novel written while he was imprisoned in St. Petersburg's Peter and Paul fortress (1863). For him and his disciples art and culture ceased to be a value in themselves; they were to be judged according to their potency as instruments in promoting a better society based upon social justice and equality.

In the 1870's the new radical youth decided to go among the (peasant) people (*narod,* hence the name *narodniki*), to enlighten and arouse them. The "people," living then in squalid, isolated villages, mostly illiterate and dull, refused to be "enlightened." In their despair some of the educated youth turned to terrorism, "the only means of self-defense and one of the most effective means of propaganda." Their victim, finally, was the Emperor himself, who was killed on a Sunday, March 13, 1881. His son and successor Alexander III (b. 1845) vigorously stamped out the revolutionary movement. The autocracy remained unshaken, the hope of a reformed and modernized Russia was not fulfilled.

Napoleon III. Different was the development in France where the liberal ideas triumphed over the popular military dictatorship established in 1852 by Napoleon III. Like his uncle in his captivity at St. Helena, the nephew liked to present himself as the friend of liberty and of a Europe united by the principle of nationality. On the strength of these "Napoleonic Ideas" (see *Absolutism and Democracy, 1815-1852,* pp. 131-133, 150-159) and as the guardian of orderly progress and religion against the threat of revolution, Prince Louis Napoleon (1808-1873) became, with the plebiscitary agreement of the masses, Emperor of the French (December 2, 1852).

By making the executive power "the beneficent motor force of the whole social order," Napoleon III preserved universal suffrage for the impotent legislative bodies. He abolished the freedom of the press and allied himself with the Catholic party to whom he abandoned the control of education. His wife, a Spanish countess, Eugénie de Montijo (1826-1920), strengthened the clerical influence which, by involvement in the Papal State and in Mexico, turned Napoleon's foreign policy into a disaster. Yet at the time of the World Fair of 1855 and the Congress of Paris (1856) and after the birth of an heir,* Napoleon III seemed to personify the example of a successful popular dictator and the permanency of the dynasty. Great public works promoted the well-being of the people.

The court life in the Tuileries Palace† was brilliant. With the help of Baron Georges Haussmann (1809-1891), prefect of the Department of the Seine (1853-1870), medieval Paris was transformed into the radiant capital of today; modern water supply and sewage systems were provided, wide tree-lined boulevards and great cross-roads squares were created, and the parks, especially the Bois de Boulogne west of the city, beautifully landscaped. Paris became an attraction for lovers of art and for tourists and the pleasure capital of the world. The operettas of Jacques Offenbach (1819-1880) and the "scandalous" can-can dance marked the gay aspect of Napoleon's reign. Gustave Flaubert (1821-1881) wrote in *Madame Bovary* the novel of provincial bourgeois boredom and the tragic attempts of the romantic heroine to escape into adulterous love, and Charles

* He died in 1879 as an officer in the British Army in the war against the Zulus in South Africa.
† The palace was burnt down during the Commune in 1871. Today a garden takes its place and perpetuates its name.

Baudelaire (1821-1867) became the father of modern poetry. His *Flowers of Evil* did not glorify the beauty of rural nature but evoked the mysteries and horrors of the big city, of poverty, loneliness, and the banality of life. Both books were made in 1857 the objects of criminal procedure on account of "obscenity."

Napoleon's Foreign Policy. The 1850's were Napoleon's best period on account of his alliance with Britain. It reached its climax in the commercial treaty between the two nations (January 5, 1860) which was negotiated by Richard Cobden. It introduced the principle of free trade on the European continent.* But soon Napoleon aroused British distrust by his involvement in Italy. His underlying ideas accorded with the trend of the time, but his ambiguities produced stresses to which the Emperor's mental and physical condition proved not equal. His identification with the Catholic interests in Rome and in Mexico and his preference, shared at that time by many French intellectuals, of Prussia over Austria, led Napoleon to his final downfall. (*See Reading No. 3.*)

National Unification of Rumania. In 1858 Rumania consisted of two (Danube) principalities, Moldavia and Wallachia, both under Turkish suzerainty. Representative bodies of the two principalities elected in January 1859 the Moldavian *boyar* (nobleman) John Cuza (1820-1873) as their prince (*hospodar*). Democratic reforms were introduced; but Cuza's highhanded methods alienated public opinion, and he was forced to abdicate in February 1866. In his stead Prince Charles of Hohenzollern-

* France, which had given the impulse to personal freedom, was able to usher in greater freedom of trade through the Napoleonic treaty system of 1860-70. England might be treated as an exception by other nations. France was always an inspiration; and, although free trade had been an accomplished fact in England in the forties, and though the European movement was based originally on English economic writers, yet it needed the French advertisement and Napoleon III to make it European. It is difficult for us to realize the glamour which this France, rejuvenated after the wars of 1815, was able to exercise on its contemporaries in the first three quarters of the nineteenth century. (L. C. A. Knowles, *Economic Development in the Nineteenth Century: France, Germany, Russia and the United States* [London: Routledge and Kegan Paul, 1932], p. 21.)

Sigmaringen (1839-1914) was elected; though he sympathized with Prussia, the French-educated elite of the country, represented by the family Bratianu, four of whom held important ministerial posts between 1867 and 1928, favored France. Napoleon had favored Rumanian unification because the people spoke a Romance language and appeared as an outpost of Latin civilization surrounded by Slav and Magyar-speaking peoples.

Italian Unification. But Napoleon was more deeply involved with the unification problems of Italy, France's "younger sister" in the Latin world. In its origins the Bonaparte family represented a link between the two foremost Latin nations. Unification was envisaged in the 1850's in the form of a federation, maintaining the various major dynasties and above all Papal rule in his state. Mazzini's struggle for a unitarian republic had become discredited by his many unsuccessful insurrections. Daniele Manin (1804-1857), the hero of the Venetian republic of 1849, Marchese Giorgio Pallavicino (1796-1878), a Lombard, and Giuseppe La Farina (1815-1863), a Sicilian, founded in 1856 the *Società Nazionale Italiana,* the Italian National Society. They co-operated with Cavour to create a unified Italy under the house of Savoy, the Kings of Sardinia. Their success in 1861, unforeseen in 1858, was a blow to Napoleon's prestige. It weakened the French leadership in the Latin world and alienated his chief support in France, the Catholic clericals who feared for the security of the Papal State in the new Italian Kingdom.

Secret Diplomacy. On July 20, 1858, Napoleon III concluded a secret treaty with Cavour at Plombières, a small hot springs resort town in the Vosges in northeastern France. It foresaw an Italian confederation under the presidency of the Pope whose territories would be confined to Latium, a mighty expansion of Piedmont as a North Italian Kingdom by the annexation of Lombardy, Venetia, Parma, Modena, and the Papal Legations; a Kingdom of Central Italy, formed by Tuscany and the Papal provinces of Umbria and the Marches and ruled by Napoleon's cousin married to a daughter of the King of Sardinia; and finally the Kingdom of Naples and Sicily. France on her part would receive the two Piedmontese frontier territories of Savoy and Nice. Cavour had to find a pretext for a war with Austria in which France would come to the help of "attacked"

Sardinia. The two plotters sought ardently for a way to provoke Austria into "aggression," and finally Austrian clumsiness played into Cavour's hands. Napoleon could now come to Cavour's help, and the French Army drove the Austrians out of Lombardy. Yet Napoleon stopped halfway. Worried about the Catholics in France and the Prussians on the Rhine, he suggested to Franz Joseph an armistice which was concluded at Villafranca near Verona on July 11, 1859, and later formalized in the peace treaty of Zurich. It confirmed Napoleon's plan for a confederation under the Pope, but with the inclusion of Austria which had only to cede Lombardy to Piedmont. Napoleon renounced the acquisition of Savoy and Nice.

Cavour, feeling betrayed by Napoleon, was now in despair; but the National Society took over and arranged for the convocation of national assemblies in Tuscany, Parma, Modena, and the Papal Romagna which voted to join Piedmont and to recognize Victor Emmanuel II, the King of Sardinia, as their ruler. The peace treaty of Zurich remained a dead letter. Napoleon dropped his objections to the creation of a unified Italy in exchange for the territories of Nice and Savoy. In the spring of 1860 central Italy voted overwhelmingly for union with Piedmont. The "legitimate" dynasties gave way before the dynamism of "revolutionary" nationalism.

Garibaldi and Southern Italy. More difficult was the problem of the Bourbon Kingdom of Naples and Sicily. The southern population showed no desire for merging with northern Piedmont. Sicily demanded its independence from Naples but did not wish to exchange it for dependence on the "alien" and unknown north. In that situation Cavour conspired with the famous guerrilla fighter and professional revolutionary Giuseppe Garibaldi (1807-1882), a native of Nice and one of the few remaining democratic romantics of 1848. With a volunteer force of about one thousand men in red shirts, he sailed from Genoa, which was since 1815 a Piedmontese port, to Sicily. By a daring use of his small force and the deceptive use of rhetoric, Garibaldi defeated the Neapolitan garrisons, made himself dictator of Sicily, and crossed the Straits of Messina into Naples. But Cavour was determined not to allow the prestige of the popular hero to raise any doubts about the primacy of the house of Savoy throughout Italy. The Sardinian army quickly moved southward along the Adriatic Sea to avoid Rome, defeated the volunteer Papal army under the French anti-Bonapartist general Louis de Lamoricière (1806-1865) at Castelfidardo near Ancona (September 18, 1860), and on November 7 King Victor Emmanuel and Garibaldi rode into Naples. (*See Reading No. 26.*)

The Unification of Italy. The Kingdom of Naples voted in a plebiscite in the fall of 1860 to join "Italy," and the Papal provinces of the Marches and Umbria were annexed the following month. Through Napoleon's halfhearted military help and Cavour's skillful and callous diplomacy, Italy was united in the spring of 1861. Only Rome, still under the Pope, and Venetia, still under the Habsburgs, remained outside for the time being. Cavour himself died before he could consolidate his system of "revolt and annexation" on June 5, 1861, at the age of fifty. For a short time Turin became the capital of Italy and the Sardinian constitution that of the united nation. Yet Piedmontese rule remained insecure in the south and was often challenged by popular insurrections and peasant unrest. Many thousands of "brigands" were shot by the Piedmontese army. Theirs was a lost cause. From the way in which Italy was unified, it suffered for many decades from its southern problem, and a wide gulf separated the more highly developed north from the underdeveloped *mezzogiorno* or south. The events of 1858 showed the acceptance of the new *Realpolitik* and the disregard for treaties solemnly signed only a short while before. The "Holy Alliance" of the monarchs had definitely given way to the new dynamism of nationalism, directed from above yet utilizing the unleashed forces of the masses. (*See Reading No. 4.*)

CHAPTER 4

Wars and Reforms, 1862-1871

Bismarck. A greater mastermind in *Realpolitik* than Cavour appeared on the stage of European history in the 1860's to dominate it for 28 years. The Prussian nobleman (*Junker*) Otto von Bismarck (1815-1898) was not, as Cavour was, a moderate liberal and a parliamentary constitutionalist but a conservative without any high regard for parliamentary institutions. Piedmont and Prussia were both frontier territories, remote from the traditional seats of Italian and German culture. Piedmont was Italy's link with the West; Prussia, Germany's northeastern part of the great East European plains. Piedmont was a small country, and its army unable to support, without foreign help, Italy's unification. Prussia was a great power with the then best army in Europe. Piedmont's capital Turin became Italy's capital only until 1864 (the center of Italy was transferred to Florence in 1864 and to Rome in 1871), and Piedmont was absorbed in Italy. Prussia's capital Berlin became in 1871 the capital of the new German *Reich,* united by Prussia, and Prussia imposed its leadership and character on the *Reich*. This Prussian Germany became under Bismarck the hegemonial European power, whereas Italy never became more than the by far weakest of the great powers.

Napoleon's Rapid Decline. Italy was united in 1861 against Napoleon's federal and pro-Papal plans. Napoleon saw himself forced to defend Papal Rome against the new Italian Kingdom, especially against Garibaldi's attempts, to repeat the model set by his Sicilian expedition. The "Roman question" undermined Franco-Italian relations throughout the 1860's. Napoleon's attempt to create a Latin and Catholic empire in the western hemisphere south of the Rio Grande during the War between the States north of the river as a counterforce to the then largely Anglo-Saxon and Protestant United States failed, and this failure undermined the last vestiges of his reputation. Supported by conservative and clerical forces in Mexico and driven on by the Empress Eugenie, Napoleon prevailed in 1863 upon the Austrian Archduke Maximilian (1832-1867), a brother of Francis Joseph, to accept an imperial crown of Mexico, offered him by a "plebiscite." With the help of a French army under Marshal Achille Bazaine (1811-1888) and the local oligarchy, the well-meaning but misguided and naive Habsburg prince could establish himself temporarily in Mexico; but he found himself in a hopeless situation when the French army was recalled in 1867, partly under American pressure and partly as a result of Prussia's victory in the war of 1866.

Maximilian refused to return to Europe with the French army and to abandon his followers. He was soon captured by the army of President Benito Pablo Juarez (1806-1872), who as a forerunner of Mexican revolutionary nationalism, tried to reduce the influence of Church and army in Mexico and to modernize the country. Maximilian's execution in Querétaro in central Mexico, northwest of Mexico City, dealt a heavy blow to Napoleon's prestige. His pro-Polish policy of 1863 antagonized Russia without helping the Poles. The domestic opposition grew, and Napoleon had to make some reluctant concessions. Finally, early in 1870 he agreed to introduce a parliamentary regime headed by Émile Ollivier (1825-1913). It was too late. In July 1870 the Empire took the fateful step of a declaration of war against Prussia, for which the foreign minister, the Duke of Gramont (1819-1880), was largely responsible. Less than two months later the Second Empire reached its end. Its gravedigger was the Emperor himself—his pro-Catholic, glory-seeking policy and his weariness caused by illness and the pleasures of life. An important factor, however, was Bismarck's superior policy and his adroit utilization of the dynamism of German nationalism.

Bismarck and German Nationalism. After the defeat suffered in 1849, German nationalism was quiescent for a decade. The example of Italy in 1859 reawakened it. A National Society was founded in Gotha, Thuringia, which strove for a parliamentary regime in a unified Germany under Prussia's leadership. Prince William (1797-1888), who had played a leading role suppressing the German revolutions of 1848/49, became Prussian regent when his brother Frederick William IV became insane in 1858, and followed him on the throne in 1861. His rise aroused hopes for a New Era of liberal reforms by which Prussia would win over the German educated middle class. But this hope was soon lost in the constitutional conflict, which arose out of the King's desire to reform and expand the army. The liberal majority of the Prussian Chamber, in which a complicated indirect voting system assured the predominance of the wealthy classes, rejected the King's demands for additional budgetary appropriations for the army. The King dissolved the Chamber. Yet the Prussian electorate returned an even greater majority of opponents to the proposed army reforms and to the strengthening of the control of the army by the King.

In that situation, the King decided at the suggestion of General Albrecht von Roon (1803-1879), Prussia's minister of war from 1859 to 1873, to invite Bismarck to become prime minister of Prussia and to carry through the army reform against the opposition of the Chamber. Bismarck accepted in September 1862 and ruled the country for the next four years, with the help of the bureaucracy, in an autocratic way. At the same time Bismarck held the portfolio of foreign minister, for which he was well prepared. From 1851 he had represented Prussia at the Diet of the German Confederation in Frankfort-on-the-Main, leading there the opposition to Austria. From 1859 on he was Prussian minister at the Court of St. Petersburg, determined on maintaining Russian-Prussian co-operation; and early in 1862 he became ambassador to France where he had the opportunity of studying the weaknesses of Napoleon III. Now, as Prussian prime minister, Bismarck challenged and incensed the German liberal and nationalist classes, who saw in him an arch-reactionary servant of Prussian interests and an enemy of German unification and parliamentary liberties. Bismarck vetoed the reforms of the German Confederation, proposed by Austria and all other major German governments. In 1863 he gave his full support to Russia in her suppression of the ill-prepared Polish struggle for national liberation, in which Western public opinion and a large majority of German Liberals sympathized with the Polish cause. Bismarck became in 1863 the most unpopular, and even hated, politician in Prussia and throughout Germany.

The War against Denmark. Bismarck showed his diplomatic superiority in the way in which he handled the problem of Schleswig-Holstein, which had agitated German nationalists as far back as 1848. They wished to separate the two duchies from Denmark and establish them as a German state. Bismarck approached the problem not from a German but from a Prussian point of view. He wished to annex the duchies to Prussia and thus gain for her an important maritime access. Of the two duchies, the southern one, Holstein, formed part of the Danish monarchy but at the same time was a member of the German Confederation; the northern one, Schleswig, was only in its southern part German-speaking and did not belong to the German Confederation or the pre-1806 *Reich*. Both duchies had been under the Danish dynasty since 1460. The future of the duchies and of Denmark, situated between the Baltic and North Seas, was of great concern to Britain and Russia; both were in favor of preserving Denmark's territorial integrity. Bismarck had to take all these various points of view into consideration, above all also Austria's objection to Prussian aggrandizement.

His opportunity came with the death of King Frederick VII of Denmark who died childless in 1863. Different laws of succession prevailed in Denmark and in the duchies. Thus Christian IX (1818-1906) of the ducal house of Schleswig-Holstein-Sonderburg-Glücksburg became King of Denmark, and Frederick VIII of Schleswig-Holstein-Sonderburg-Augustenburg (in brief "the Augustenburger," 1829-1880) claimed the succession in the duchies. His claims were recognized by the Diet of the German Confederation and the German national movement and, initially, also by Bismarck. Bismarck succeeded in enlisting Austria's participation in a war against Denmark for the duchies which bordered on Prussia but were very far away from Austria. After a very short and inexpensive war in 1864, Denmark ceded the two duchies to Prussia and Austria.

Bismarck now openly rejected the claims of the Augustenburger. On his suggestion the administration of the two duchies was divided between Prussia and Austria, which as could be foreseen led to steady friction between the two powers. In 1866 Bismarck felt the time ripe for a complete reform of the German Confederation by the exclusion of Austria and the creation of a German parliament elected by universal suffrage. He had learned

from Napoleon III that a democratically elected legislative body
could be manipulated by a strong authoritarian executive. He
hoped that his "democratic" proposal would win him the support of the German Liberal Nationalists. It did not then.
Bismarck continued to be the most widely distrusted German
politician. (*See Reading No. 5.*)

Prussia's War against the German Confederation. Bismarck was quite alone in his decision to start a German civil
war. The German Confederation and all the German middle
states sided with Austria. Even in Prussia and in the royal family
Bismarck met with strong opposition. But he had laid his plans
carefully and with psychological understanding. He concluded
an alliance with Italy against Austria and resorted to subversive
propaganda among Hungarians and Czechs, the discontented
nationalities of the Habsburg monarchy. Though the Austrians
under Archduke Albert (1817-1895) defeated the Italians decisively on land at Custozza near Verona and on sea under
Admiral Wilhelm von Tegetthoff (1827-1871) at Lissa, an
Adriatic island today called Vis, they had promised to Napoleon
III as a condition of his neutrality in the war to cede Venetia to
Italy irrespective of the military decisions. The diplomacy of
Napoleon III and of Francis Joseph was much inferior to that
of Bismarck and assured his success. It strengthened the belief
among the Germans that their leaders would always surpass their
adversaries, that the outcome of the decisive year of 1866 was
not due to possibly changing circumstances but to the innate
and institutional superiority of Prussia's military monarchy.

The great triumph of Bismarck and Prussia came quickly on
Austria's northern front. The middle states were unprepared
and did not sufficiently co-operate, so that Prussia could easily
overrun Hanover and Bavaria. The Austrian army (together
with the Saxon army) met the Prussian army on July 3 at
Königgrätz (Sadowa) in eastern Bohemia. The Austrians were
under the command of Ludwig August von Benedek (1804-
1881), a general whose military experience was limited to the
Italian battlefields and who assumed the command of the
Bohemian army only on the Emperor's explicit order and had
to count with Vienna's interference. The victorious Prussian
army was directed by Helmuth von Moltke (1800-1891), chief

of the Prussian general staff from 1858 to 1888. In view of the difficulties of transferring the Austrian army from Italy to Bohemia, no forces were available to stop the Prussian march on Vienna. Bismarck, however, was eager to make peace as fast as possible and, against the will of his generals, did impose no territorial losses on Austria.

The Peace Treaty of Prague. The treaty dissolved the German Confederation of 1815. The hold of Prussia on northern Germany was strengthened by large-scale annexations. Though a professed monarchist, Bismarck disregarded legitimate and long-established dynastic rights. The Kingdom of Hanover, the duchies of Schleswig-Holstein in the north and of Nassau in the west, the Electorate of Hessen-Kassel, and the Free City of Frankfort-on-the-Main, the former coronation place of the German-Roman emperors and the seat of the Diet of the German Confederation and of the National Assembly of 1848, became part of Prussia.* Bismarck treated the Free City of Frankfort with a special animosity. The remaining states of northern Germany (including the Kingdom of Saxony) were organized into a North-German Confederation of princes under the leadership of the King of Prussia. Bismarck remained Prussian Prime Minister and became the Chancellor of the Confederation. The power of the Crown remained supreme, as it was in Prussia, and the cabinet was responsible only to the Monarch; but for legislative purposes a democratically elected *Bundestag* based on general suffrage was instituted. Besides the *Bundestag,* representing the population, there was a *Bundesrat* (in both cases in 1871 the word *Bund* was replaced by *Reich*), representing the various governments in the *Bund* but retaining a clear preponderance of Prussia. The four South German states, south of the Main River, of which Bavaria was the largest, became fully independent but concluded secret military alliances with Prussia in case of war with France. In addition, the Customs Union was strengthened by allowing a customs parliament, which included the southern states, to act by majority vote. Thus the

---

* In the Treaty of Prague the population of northern Schleswig received the right to decide by a plebiscite whether it wished to join Denmark or Prussia. This right could be exercised only in 1920, after the Treaty of Versailles (1919) confirmed it.

"independent" southern states lost their decision-making power in foreign affairs and foreign trade policy to Prussian leadership.

The Consequences of 1866. The consequences of the year 1866 determined European history for the next half century. Most German Liberals who had been hostile to Bismarck capitulated. After all, he and the Prussian military caste had realized the Liberals' hope of 1848, German unity, German power, and a more or less liberal constitution. They became the greatest admirers of the "Iron Chancellor" and of his methods, and their nationalism gratefully accepted authority from above and the preponderant role of the army in national life, a role they had twice rejected only four years ago. Four years later, when Bismarck crowned his work by victory over France, then the "hereditary enemy," the national liberals, saw the year 1871 as the realization of the hopes of the War of Liberation of 1813. The events of 1848/49 appeared to the new German historiography as an unessential and untoward incident in the steep rise from the dissolution of the powerless old *Reich* in 1806 to the immense power of the new German *Reich*.

As a consequence of the events of 1866, Francis Joseph was now ready to accept most of Hungary's demands for the independence of the Kingdom of the Hungarian Crown from Austria. Within the historical boundaries of this Kingdom, the non-Magyar nationalities forming the majority of the population were sacrificed to the leadership of the Magyar nobility. Only the Croatians preserved, for historical reasons, a measure of autonomy. Francis Deák (1803-1876) gained the restoration of the Hungarian constitution on the basis of complete parity with all the other parts of the Habsburg lands, which though much superior in population and economic development were too little unified not to have to cede much of a real parity to the Hungarian partner. The "Compromise" (*Ausgleich*) of 1867 created the Dual Monarchy of Austria-Hungary in which Francis Joseph was Emperor of Austria and King of Hungary. Only three resorts were common to both parts and administered by imperial and royal (*Kaiserliche und Königliche*) ministers— foreign affairs, defense, and the appropriations needed to finance these two resorts.

All other possibly common interests (customs, communications, etc.) had to be legislated every ten years by delegations of the two parliaments, constituted on a basis of complete equality. Again, the Hungarian delegation could speak with a united voice, pushing Hungary's demands, whereas the Austrian could not. The looseness of the Austrian half of the Dual Monarchy was visible in its official name, "The Kingdoms and lands represented in the *Reichsrat*," the parliament introduced by the Austrian constitution of 1867. But there was no possibility of transforming this looseness into a real federal structure. The Magyars under the leadership of Count Julius Andrássy (1823-1880), who became in 1867 Hungary's first constitutional prime minister, opposed the introduction of federalism in Austria. They feared that such a step might arouse similar demands among the nationalities in Hungary. To make Magyar supremacy in Hungary secure, Andrássy wished to preserve the supremacy of the German element in Austria (and of the Poles in the Austrian province of Galicia). The Austrian constitution of 1867 was far from democratic in its suffrage, but generally liberal in its outlook and proclaimed the equality of all nationalities and the rights of the citizens to use their own language in education and in public life. But "the advent of dualism made impossible in the Danube basin the development of that free collaboration of peoples of different language and race that took place in Switzerland." * The dualism which Andrássy promoted became after only half a century the gravedigger not only of the Dual Monarchy but also of the historical Kingdom of Hungary. Another factor contributing to this catastrophe was the foreign policy of the Dual Monarchy, the foundations of which were again laid by Andrássy in what he regarded as Hungary's anti-Russian and anti-Slav interest.

Austro-Hungarian Foreign Policy. From 1867 to 1870 Francis Joseph did not abandon the hope of restoring the ancient Habsburg position in Germany. To that end Count Friedrich Ferdinand von Beust (1809-1886), who had been the pro-Austrian and anti-Prussian Saxon foreign minister from 1853 to 1866, was called to Vienna as foreign minister. Little interested in Austro-Hungarian internal affairs, he easily aban-

* Robert C. Binkley, *Realism and Nationalism 1852-1871* (New York: Harper Torchbooks), p. 279.

doned Austrian rights to Hungarian pressure in order to win
Magyar support for his foreign policy. Yet, soon it became clear
that the anti-Prussian foreign policy led nowhere. In 1866
Napoleon III had expected a long war between Prussia and
Austria in which he could ultimately play the role of a mediator.
The Prussian victory at Königgrätz came unexpectedly fast and
was felt by many Frenchmen to be as much a French as an
Austrian defeat. Napoleon's clumsy efforts to receive com-
pensations for Prussia's aggrandizement were easily thwarted
by Bismarck and turned against Napoleon. Austrian efforts to
conclude an alliance with France, and perhaps Italy, were partly
frustrated by the Hungarians who had no interest in restoring
Habsburg influence in Germany and by the Austrian Germans,
the leading nationality in the non-Hungarian Habsburg lands,
who refused to support Napoleon III against Germany. Thus,
the events of 1866 strengthened Prussia beyond all expectation,
converted the German Liberals to the acceptance of an authoritarian state, started the disintegration of the Habsburg monarchy
by impeding a federal solution there, and decisively weakened
Napoleon III and France. All these trends were confirmed by
the outcome of the Franco-Prussian War of 1870.

The Franco-Prussian War.   In spite of its short duration,
this war was the most embittered nationalist struggle in Europe
between 1815 and 1914. The bitterness was a consequence of
the war of liberation against Napoleon I and a prelude to World
War I. Throughout the nineteenth century the Rhine frontier
was contested between Germans and Frenchmen. The Germans
enthusiastically mounted the "guard on the Rhine" (*Die Wacht
am Rhein*). At that time little inclination existed, certainly none
on the part of Bismarck, to expand Germany eastward. The
existence of the Russian and Habsburg empires made such an
expansion most doubtful. This situation changed only in the
second decade of the twentieth century.

The Franco-Prussian War inaugurated, as a result of the
humiliating peace imposed upon France, the era of the "armed
peace" in Europe, of steadily mounting armaments and military
budgets, and of a system of alliances which originated in Bismarck's fear of France escaping from her diplomatic isolation.
Yet the immediate "cause" of this fateful war was insignificant.

When Queen Isabella of Spain (1830-1904) was deposed by an uprising against her misrule in 1868, the throne was offered to Prince Leopold of Hohenzollern-Sigmaringen (1835-1905) of the southern and Catholic branch of the house ruling in Prussia. The French feared this "encirclement" which recalled to them the one by the house of Habsburg in the sixteenth century.

Prince Leopold withdrew his candidacy, but the French foreign minister ordered the French minister to the Prussian court, Count Vincente Benedetti (1817-1900), to ask King William, who was vacationing in the resort town of Ems east of the Rhine, for a solemn renunciation of the Prince's candidacy (July 13, 1870). The King refused and wired an account of his interview to Bismarck, who was dining that evening with Moltke and Roon. Bismarck shortened the telegram to make it sound more abrupt and offensive for the French and gave it to the press. Moltke and Roon were highly pleased because they expected that the French would react in a bellicose way. This did happen: France declared war on Prussia on July 19th. The South-German states, in fulfillment of their secret military alliances, joined Prussia. French efforts to seek Austrian and Italian support were fruitless, partly because the time was so short, partly because French protection of Papal Rome alienated Italy's sympathy for France. (*See Reading No. 6.*)

The Course of the War. Germans and French greeted the war with enthusiasm, an enthusiasm repeated in 1914. But the incompetence and unpreparedness of the French army command lost the war in a very short time. One French army under Bazaine was encircled in the fortress of Metz in the Moselle River valley. The other under Marshal Count Maurice Mac-Mahon (1808-1893), which hastened to Bazaine's help instead of protecting the road to Paris, was encircled by the Germans at Sedan, a city on the Meuse River near the Belgian border. The Emperor was with his army. On September 2 he and the army surrendered to the Germans. The day of Sedan was gaily celebrated every year in Germany until the dreadful seriousness of the consequences of Sedan and of war itself became manifest in the course of the War of 1914.

Two days after the surrender the Second Empire came to an end. On September 4 the Republicans in Paris organized a

Government of National Defense. At the end of September the Germans reached Paris and started the siege of the city. Léon Gambetta (1838-1882), a Republican leader who had opposed the declaration of war but urged its vigorous prosecution once it had started, left in a balloon to raise new armies in the provinces. Paris resisted heroically until after four months of hunger forced it to surrender. An armistice was signed on January 28, 1871, by Jules Favre (1809-1880), and elections were held for a National Assembly to ratify the peace treaty. The Assembly met in Bordeaux in southwestern France and elected Adolphe Thiers (1797-1877, see *Absolutism and Democracy 1814-1852*, p. 90) as head of state. The Republicans formed only a small minority of the Assembly.

The German Reich. Bismarck's overwhelming diplomatic and military victory made him not only the idol of the German middle class and intellectuals but made the foundation of the (Second) German *Reich* possible, nay inevitable. It was a *Reich* very different from the first one which ended in 1806. The first one was anchored in the west and south of Germany where in Roman times cities were founded as centers of Western civilization. The new *Reich* in which Prussia was dominant, gravitated to the northeast, to formerly Slav territories conquered by German invaders in the later Middle Ages. This new *Reich* was not created, as the new Italy at least formally was, by plebiscites or parliamentary decisions, but by military power and by the German princes. The most important among them, after the King of Prussia, was King Louis II of Bavaria of the ancient house of Wittelsbach, who ruled from 1864 to 1886. He was brought in only by Bismarck's heavy pressure. Assembled in the Hall of Mirrors of the French royal palace of Versailles, at the gates of the besieged enemy capital, the princes and generals—there were no persons in civilian attire present—proclaimed King William I of Prussia German Emperor. The date was carefully chosen; it was January 18, 1871, the 170th anniversary of the day on which the Elector of Brandenburg Frederick I assumed the title of King of Prussia in Königsberg (Mount Royal), the most northeastern city of Prussia and an important port on the Baltic Sea surrounded by Polish and Lithuanian populations. Today Königsberg has disappeared from the maps. The land forms a part of the Soviet Union, and the city is called Kaliningrad.* In 1871 Berlin became, for the first time in history, the capital of Germany. The constitution of the North German Confederation was altered to correspond to the new situation. Bavaria and Württemberg, the two South German Kingdoms, were allowed to retain some of the attributes of their former sovereignty.

Peace-Making. The negotiations for peace between Bismarck and Thiers provided for the payment, on the part of the French, of an indemnity of five billion gold francs, very much more than the cost of the war for Germany. Bismarck and the German generals received handsome donations. The three wars fought by Prussia within six years seemed to prove that wars carefully prepared do pay. Part of France was to be occupied until the full payment of the indemnity. The French resented above all the cession of Alsace (inhabited largely by German-speaking French citizens) and of part of (French-speaking) Lorraine, including the fortress of Metz. The deputies of Alsace-Lorraine in the French National Assembly declared unanimously "null and void the pact that disposes of us without our consent." The Germans maintained that the Alsatians were Germans by descent and had therefore to belong to their "true" homeland; the Alsatians countered with the claims that whatever their past, their present free decision made them French. The Alsatians continued to adhere to this point of view until the end of World War I. Many political observers of 1871 believed that this German territorial conquest made war between Germany and France in the future inevitable. The peace was signed in Frankfort-on-the-Main on May 10, 1871. On the Place de la Concorde, the central square of Paris, adorned by statues representing the principal cities of France, the statue of Strasbourg remained draped in deep black until 1918.

Social Revolution. Meanwhile, however, the workers and artisans of Paris, who felt betrayed by the Assembly's readiness to accept the terms of peace, decided to reject the peace treaty and the conservative Assembly. The Parisian National Guard

* Mikhail Kalinin (1875-1946), a Russian of peasant origin, filled the place of the head of state in the Soviet Union 1919-1946. Königsberg was renamed after him in 1946.

called for the election of a Municipal Council to organize the resistance. The revolutionary movement behind the Commune owed as much to patriotic fervor as to socialist hopes. There was no clear program or leadership. Many of the workers were republicans, rightly suspecting the National Assembly of wishing to restore the monarchy. Most of the Socialists were under the influence of Pierre Joseph Proudhon (1809-1865). They were federalists, rejected Marx's centralization of power, and thought of a decentralized France based on freely co-operating municipalities.

The poorly organized defense of the capital, besieged this time by the largely monarchist army of Thiers, collapsed after two months on May 28. In its last days, as a reprisal, the Commune executed some hostages, among them the Archbishop of Paris. In counteraction, the victorious army of the National Assembly massacred a very large though undetermined number of the defenders of Paris; others were sentenced to deportation or long terms of imprisonment. The way in which the Commune was repressed was even more than the repression of the Parisian workers in June 1848, a sign of the hardening of class warfare. The War of 1870/71 ended on an ominous note for the peace between the two leading continental nations and for the peaceful adjustment of the tensions arising from the industrial revolution.

CHAPTER 5

Post-1870 France and Germany

The two leading continental nations followed opposite paths of internal development after 1871. In France, in spite of many contrary trends, a democratic republic gained in strength, whereas in Germany the conservative and authoritarian forces prevailed. Democracy in France was never based, as it is in Britain, Switzerland, or the United States, on a general consensus. There were always two Frances: the one originating in 1789, the other looking nostalgically back to the *ancien régime*. From time to time the republic passed through crises which threatened to reintroduce an authoritarian regime based upon the Army and the Church. Nevertheless, for seventy years the Third Republic overcame these crises and lasted until 1940. It provided France with the most stable government known in her history between 1789 and 1958. From 1879 to 1917 France was the only republic among the larger European states.

The Birth of the Third Republic. In 1871 such a development in France was in no way certain. Thiers' first concern was to pay the (for that time) enormous indemnity and to end the occupation of French provinces by the Germans. He succeeded in an astonishingly short time. By 1873 the indemnity was paid and Thiers could retire. Though a lifelong adherent of the Orleanist dynasty which had ruled France from 1830 to 1848 (see *Absolutism and Democracy, 1814-1852,* p. 90f.), he had become a moderate republican because the "republic divides us least." But his republic was a conservative republic, led by the "notables," the great bourgeois families of France. He was followed by the imperial Marshal MacMahon. His election, following the collapse of the empire, a thorough military defeat and a social uprising, can be compared to the election of the imperial Field Marshal Paul von Hindenburg under similar circumstances in Germany in 1925. Here, however, the similarities end. MacMahon was forced to resign and to make way for a thoroughly republican government; Hindenburg was the link between the dynastic empire and the triumph of National Socialism which he made possible.

The Monarchists in the Assembly were divided into three factions: the legitimists, the adherents of the older line of the Bourbons which had ended with the fall of Charles X in 1830; the Orleanists who looked to the progeny of the "bourgeois king" Louis Philippe; and the imperialists who expected the "prince imperial," Napoleon III's son, living in England, to regain the throne for the Bonaparte dynasty. The majority of the Chamber agreed to offer the crown first to Henri, Count of Chambord (1820-1883), the grandson of Charles X and the only surviving member of the older royal line who lived in Austria. Being an elderly man and without children, the crown after his death would fall to the pretender of the house of Orleans, Louis Philippe, Count of Paris (1838-1894). The Count of Chambord, an outspoken adherent of the principle of divine right, made his acceptance depend on the abandonment of the tricolor which had been not only the flag of the revolution but also of the Orleans and Bonaparte dynasties. The Chamber, however, balked at the reintroduction of the white flag with the fleur-de-lys.

Meanwhile, the Chamber decided upon a "provisional" constitution, which adopted in 1875 remained in power until 1940. It fixed the term of the President for seven years, provided for a Chamber of Deputies elected by universal suffrage and for a Senate elected indirectly in a rather complex manner and assuring a strong representation of rural France. The elections of the Chamber in 1876 resulted in a republican majority so that a monarchist President, Senate, and bureaucracy faced a republican Chamber. The following confrontation of the two forces ended in 1879 with the victory of republicanism. The constitutional struggle was similar to that fought out in Prussia between 1862 and 1866. But this time democracy won. On May 16 (*le seize mai*) 1877 MacMahon imitated the Prussian King. He dismissed the constitutional ministry which had the backing of the Chamber and appointed one of his own choice. He dissolved the Chamber; but in spite of all the efforts of the Church and of the monarchists, the new Chamber in 1877 showed an even greater republican majority. MacMahon ceded and appointed a republican ministry. In 1878 new elections to the Senate resulted in a republican majority in the Upper Chamber, too, and in 1879 MacMahon resigned. The new President, elected by both Houses, meeting together for that purpose, was a republican, Jules Grévy (1807-1891). The Third Republic came thus into its own in 1879. The Chamber of Deputies became, like the House of Commons in Britain, the center of sovereignty. In both countries the cabinets expressed the will of the majority party or coalition of the democratically elected Chamber. The President became as limited in his powers as was the monarch in the United Kingdom.

French Revival. The new republican administration restored July 14, the day of the capture of the Bastille in 1789, as a national holiday and transferred the capital from Versailles with its monarchist memories to Paris, the city of revolution and the people. In 1872 the French Army was reorganized on the Prussian model of universal military service. Universal compulsory and free elementary education were introduced on a secular patriotic basis under Jules Ferry (1832-1893) as Minister of Education. At the same time France revived economically in a very short time. The French Revolution had solved the agrarian problem in France. Most peasants had become proprietors and, living in a frugal or even parsimonious way, were able to save money. Together with the petite bourgeoisie they invested it largely in government bonds. Literature and art flourished. Émile Zola (1840-1902) described in the naturalistic manner of a social scientist in his Rougon-Macquart series of novels "the natural and social history of a family living under the Second Empire." He was a close friend of the new school of painters called "impressionists," especially of Edouard Manet (1832-1883). Zola's sharp reaction against industrial and financial capitalism was shared by Honoré Daumier (1808-1879) who drew satirical cartoons for the widely read *Charivari*.

Paris assumed under the Third Republic the leading position in the visual arts which had once been held by Italy and later by the Netherlands. In spite of domestic quarrels and a certain instability of the cabinets (which was, however, mitigated by the permanency of a highly trained and centralized bureaucracy, the heritage of the great monarchs and of Napoleon I), the Third Republic added to the glories of France and made it in the later half of the nineteenth century the "second homeland" of every (liberal) European (or South American). The great expositions in Paris in 1878, and then in 1889 and in 1900, contributed to the spread of French fame.

Germany after 1871. Different was the development in Germany. In the second half of the nineteenth century, in spite of its military and political triumphs, Germany played hardly any role in world literature or in the visual arts. Only in music German composers continued their great creativity. Richard Wagner (1813-1883) and Johannes Brahms (1833-1897), who opposed each other bitterly, were the leading representatives of the period. Wagner, a firebrand in his youth, who had participated in the Revolution of 1849 and was then exiled from Germany, came back in 1864 upon the invitation of a royal patron, the eighteen-year-old King Louis II of Bavaria. Wagner's reputation soon overcame the opposition to his great music-dramas, for which he wrote also the text and for the presentation of which he built a special theatre in Bayreuth in northeastern Bavaria, exclusively dedicated to Wagner festivals. It was opened in 1876 with the four evenings cycle of "Der Ring des Nibelungen," a mighty epos reviving pre-Christian Germanic myths and sagas and filling them with a deep sense of nihilism and pessimism. Brahms, who though born in Hamburg lived his mature life in Vienna, did not write for the stage but followed the older tradition in his symphonies, chamber music, and *Lieder*.

For twenty years Bismarck overshadowed the political life of Germany. With great dexterity he played the several parties of the *Reichstag* against each other, creating coalitions or blocs from case to case to support his policy. Whereas Bismarck declared himself satisfied with the hegemonial position of Germany in Europe and proclaimed Germany "satiated" and therefore adverse to all adventures in foreign policies, he applied after 1871 the ruthless methods used in his foreign policy from 1863 to 1871, in the domestic field. The most important party in the first decade of the *Reich* were the National-Liberals, who were more nationalist than liberal, the word "liberal" meaning opposition to clerical influences and promotion of private capitalistic enterprise. The party supported Bismarck throughout the decade. The German constitution and social structure did not favor the emergence of great parliamentary leaders; it was the misfortune of the German middle class not to produce a man of the stature of a Gladstone or Gambetta or even of a Cavour or Masaryk.

The "Kulturkampf." A foremost concern of many Germans after 1871 was the unity of the newly created *Reich*. They saw it threatened by many domestic enemies. Very large component parts of the German population appeared as subversive adversaries; whoever disagreed with the official policy appeared as a traitor to the *Reich*, as "un-German." The first victims of this narrow nationalism were the Roman Catholics. The *Reich* was created in the two wars of Protestant Prussia against Catholic Austria and Catholic France. The then reigning Pope had stressed the Church's rejection of modern civilization and its superiority above the State. Was there no reason to doubt the loyalty of the Roman Catholics who were accustomed to look *ultra montes* (beyond the mountains) to Rome instead of to Protestant Berlin? Did the Catholics in Bavaria, in Alsace, in Prussia's eastern provinces with their Polish population not support separatism? That all German Catholics loyally supported the *Reich*, Bismarck did not wish to acknowledge. He proclaimed the *Kulturkampf* (struggle for modern civilization and for a truly non-Romanized German culture) not out of religious but out of political motives. The Jesuits were expelled from Germany; the "May laws" of 1873-1875 put the education and appointment of Catholic priests in Prussia under state control; the compulsory civil marriage was introduced, and many religious orders were suppressed.

The German Catholics resisted. The Center Party, founded as a purely religious party representing Catholics of all classes (hence the name; the party claimed to be socially neither of the Right nor of the Left), grew rapidly in strength. The intransigent Pope Pius IX died in 1878. He was followed by Leo XIII (1810-1903), who though as deeply committed to ultramontanism as Pius IX, showed greater diplomatic skill (and also more interest in scholarship and in the situation of the working class) than his predecessor. He brought about not only a rapprochement of French Catholics with the Third Republic, the *ralliement*, but concluded an agreement with Bismarck, which led to a repeal of much of the anti-Catholic legislation. The Center Party became the strongest single party in the German *Reichstag* and began to support Bismarck.

The Turn to the Right.   The year 1879 which established the Third Republic on a firm foundation, witnessed a definite turn in Germany to the Right, a position which endured until 1917. The big industrialists and the big landowners who formed the backbone of the Conservative Party engineered the transition from a relatively liberal free trade policy to an extreme protectionism. The Catholics, being no longer the "enemies of the *Reich*," were replaced in this function by the rapidly growing Social Democrats, an attitude which lasted not only until 1917 but into the Second World War and even beyond.

The Anti-Socialist Legislation.   From 1878 to 1890 Bismarck tried to destroy the influence of Social Democracy in Germany. He, and the German upper classes, not only looked down upon the working class and its representatives, but feared their internationalism, their connection with socialists outside Germany. In 1871 the two lonely representatives of the Social Democratic Party in the German parliament, August Bebel and Karl Liebknecht, had voted against the annexation of Alsace-Lorraine. In the following years the party grew; in the election of 1877 it received 493,000 votes and held twelve seats.* Bismarck and the upper classes were deeply worried. They branded the Socialists as "enemies of the *Reich*" and "fellows without a fatherland." In 1878 two attempts at the life of Emperor William I, in no way inspired by the Socialist Party, provided the opportunity to adopt "Exceptional Laws," forbidding Socialist agitation. The police received special power to deal with Socialist "subversion" of the existing semi-autocracy. The German Socialists, little given to violence, continued a peaceful "underground" activity and the anti-Socialist laws were not renewed in 1890, the year of Bismarck's dismissal.

---

* It grew rapidly thereafter, to 1,427,000 votes and thirty-five seats in 1890 and 4,250,000 votes and 110 seats in 1912 when it became the strongest single party. By that time it had lost its internationalist character and had fully accepted the annexation of Alsace-Lorraine and German domination in the eastern Polish-speaking provinces of Prussia.

Of more lasting effect were Bismarck's positive attempts to win the workers for the existing order. Not being a liberal, but like all *Junkers* a paternalist, he introduced in 1883, 1884 and 1889 a "new deal" legislation, urged upon him by some German professors of economy, the *Kathedersozialisten,* who rejected *laissez-faire* in favor of a limited form of state-socialism.* The new laws dealt with sickness and accident insurance and finally with old-age and invalidity assurance. The insurance was obligatory and the workers, the employers, and the government contributed in varying degrees. The State thus became a benefactor of the industrial working class and gave the proletariat a new feeling of security. "It should be our aim to spread the idea among the non-propertied classes who form at once the most numerous and the least instructed part of the population, that the State is not merely a necessary but a beneficent institution. If direct benefits are secured to these classes by legislation, they will not regard it [the state] as a contrivance for the benefit only of the better classes, but as an institution serving their own needs and interests."

Bismarck's words revealed the condescension of his social attitude. He was mistaken in his belief that the state-benefits would make the worker immune against social democracy. But his social reforms were soon widely accepted in all industrially advanced countries, and the International Labor Office, established in the peace treaties of Paris (1919), extended the concern for the well-being of the workers even to less developed countries. By then, however, and throughout the twentieth century, these benefits were not dispensed by a paternalistic state in the struggle against socialism, but often by socialist and workers governments as a fundamental human right, steadily expanded and continued and improved even under "capitalistic" or right-wing governments.

Economic Progress. After 1871, and partly with the help of the indemnity paid by France, Germany underwent a rapid process of industrialization which at the beginning of the twenti-

* The foremost representatives of this school were Adolph Wagner (1835-1917) and Gustav Schmoller (1838-1917). Both were professors at the University of Berlin; Wagner was a leading member of Stöcker's Christian-Social Party and an anti-Semite.

eth century made her a successful rival of Britain, formerly *the* workshop of the world, and of the rapidly rising United States. Germany was the first country to put systematic scientific research into the service of industry and of agriculture. She became a leader in the chemical and electric industries and in shipbuilding. But only after 1879, and even more after Bismarck's dismissal in 1890, did this new economic strength of Germany with its two principal centers on the Ruhr, a right bank contributary of the Rhine, and in Upper Silesia, on the border of the then Russian-dominated Poland, directly influence its policy, its desire to become a *Weltmacht,* a world power.

The Rise of Anti-Semitism. It is not without interest to note that in 1879, when Bismarck's government took a sharp turn to the Right, abandoning the semi-liberal principles which it had followed to attract the German middle classes, anti-Semitism emerged for the first time as a major organized force. The Prussian Court Chaplain Adolf Stöcker (1835-1909) founded in Berlin the Christian-Social movement against the corruption which, according to him, Judaism carried into German life. In 1880 the Prussian high-school teacher Bernhard Förster organized a petition to be presented to Bismarck, which was signed by 250,000 persons and which demanded the exclusion of Jews from all public offices. Though not expressly demanded in the petition, it was made clear in the speeches in the mass meetings that the racial character of the Jews endangered German culture and religion and that it was desirable to revoke the emancipation and legal equality of the Jews. The Prussian government rejected this demand. Bismarck himself was no anti-Semite, but he was willing to use and manipulate anti-Semitism, as he did with many other issues, for his political aims.

More important than these "popular" movements was the impression left on the minds of the younger academic generation by the stand taken by the then most renowned and admired German historian, Heinrich von Treitschke (1834-1896), professor at Berlin University, who declared in 1879 "The Jews are our misfortune." Though Treitschke was opposed by the equally famous historian, Theodor Mommsen (1817-1903), the foremost student of Roman history and Treitschke's colleague at Berlin University, the academic youth in its vast majority followed Treitschke and his rejection of the ideals of the Enlightenment, of humanitarianism, and of emancipation. Treitschke—and to a lesser degree Richard Wagner—made anti-Semitism in which Treitschke saw "a passionate movement" of his time respectable among Germany's educated and academic circles. This agitation and the often contemptuous rejection of Western Enlightenment and emancipation bore full fruit only after 1932 in a way which probably neither Treitschke nor Stöcker would have approved.

CHAPTER 6

Disraeli and Gladstone

The years between 1852 and 1879 witnessed the greatest progress in British economy. Britain was then not only the workshop and forge but also the carrier for the world. It led all other countries in textiles, iron and steel production, and in shipbuilding. London was then the world capital for banking and insurance. From London investment capital went out to all the continents and built railroads and modernized economies. But this period was not only one of unprecedented economic growth; it was also the time of two unusual political leaders.

Disraeli. Benjamin Disraeli (1804-1881), whose parents were of Italian descent and of the Jewish faith, and who himself was baptized in his youth into the Church of England, became the great reformer of the Tory (Conservative) Party. He was a unique phenomenon among his fellow party members, much more of a romantic and yet much more in touch with the new social reality emerging in the industrial society of the century than the stolid squires were. He wrote ten novels, which were rather discussions of political problems than works of art. The two most famous appeared in 1844 and 1845, *Coningsby or the New Generation* and *Sybil or the Two Nations*. The subtitles are indicative of their contents and aims. Here spoke the most authentic voice of Young England, which sought new directions for the Tory party caught in its mediocrity and routine. Disraeli demanded from the Tories an interest in the industrial working class, its misery and potential strength, and asked for the integration of the poor into the mainstream of national life, to form one nation instead of the two nations. In the 1840's the rich and the poor faced each other across an unbridged and apparently unbridgeable abyss.*

* "Two nations," Disraeli wrote, "between whom there is no intercourse and no sympathy; who are as ignorant of each other's habits, thoughts and feelings as if they were dwellers in different zones, or inhabitants of different planets; who are formed

The Second Reform Bill. As a member of the Tory Cabinet of the fourteenth Earl of Derby (1799-1869), Disraeli in 1867 introduced a second parliamentary Reform Bill, which Gladstone had in vain demanded before. (*See Reading No. 7.*) It enlarged the electorate to include the urban working class; all householders and those who rented rooms for not less than fifty dollars a year were entitled to vote. The number of voters was thereby doubled as compared with the Reform Bill of 1832. Even in the countryside many tenant farmers were enfranchised. The opponents of the bill characterized it as a "leap in the dark," but the courageous leap helped to preserve orderly evolutionary development in Britain.

Palmerston. Yet Disraeli's interests were mainly in the field of foreign policy, as they had been in the case of Viscount Palmerston (1784-1865), a leader of the Liberal Party, who had been twice Prime Minister, 1855 to 1858 and 1859 to 1865. He was a typical Englishman of the early Victorian age, with a sure instinct for the imperialist inclinations of the masses. An old-fashioned Whig rather than a Liberal, he had little sympathy for reformers or "idealists," but he supported in common with the Liberals the wars of liberation and the Liberal "subversive" activities of nationalist agitators on the continent of Europe when he thought that they counterbalanced the power of the Holy Alliance. His forceful eloquence and caustic wit, his frequent rudeness thought typical of the country squire, made him widely popular. But he was fundamentally different from the mid-Victorian generation of Disraeli and Gladstone. In the Crimean War Palmerston defended Turkey against Russia, and in the American War between the States he sided with the South, disagreeing therein with "idealists" like John Bright, who strongly favored the North in spite of the "cotton famine" among the Lancashire workers brought about by the war. (*See Reading No. 8.*)

Gladstone. The two great men of the mid-Victorian era, Disraeli and William Ewart Gladstone (1809-1898), had little in common. Gladstone, though he became a Liberal, was a much more typical upper-class Englishman of his time than

by a different breeding, are fed by a different food, are ordered by different manners, and are governed by the same laws."

Disraeli was. The son of a very prosperous Liverpool merchant of Scot origin, Gladstone followed the normal course of education of his class and won high distinction as a student in Oxford, where, as a devout member of the Church of England, he thought of taking orders. (*See Reading No. 9.*) Disraeli had difficulties to win and to hold his first seat in Parliament; Gladstone had none. He entered the House of Commons as a Tory in 1833 at the age of twenty-four, one year after the passing of the Reform Bill, and remained with one short break a member for sixty-one years until 1894 when he withdrew in his eighty-fifth year. His unusual capacities brought him at the early age of twenty-five the first appointments in the Conservative administration of Sir Robert Peel. Gladstone became Lord of the Treasury in 1834 and Undersecretary for the Colonies in 1835. In the second administration of Sir Robert (1841-1845), Gladstone was president of the Board of Trade. In that capacity he inaugurated the policy of free trade, supported by Richard Cobden and John Bright. In the Conservative administration of the fourth Earl of Aberdeen (1784-1860), who was prime minister from 1852 to 1855, Gladstone held the very high cabinet post of Chancellor of the Exchequer. On April 18, 1853, he introduced his first budget in a speech which showed his unsurpassed grasp of the complicated problems of public finance and of domestic and colonial administration. (*See Reading No. 10.*) His budget, which was only the first of the several which he prepared, "tended to make life easier and cheaper for large and numerous classes; it promised wholesale remission of taxation; it lessened the charges on common processes of business, on locomotion, on postal communication, and on legacy-duty to real property."

In 1867 he became leader of the Liberal Party in the House of Commons. His Christian piety remained unshaken during his whole life as did his reverence for the conservative pillars of the Establishment of the period—the Monarchy, the Church, and the Universities. To his deep immersion in the classical literatures of Greece and Rome and in the Old and New Testament, not only his parliamentary speeches bore witness but also his profuse though hardly legible writings on Homeric and Biblical themes, for which he found time even during the busy years of his devotion to public life. This combination of an unusually well-grounded education in the humanities with a perhaps inherited practical sense of economics and economy, of a deep religious feeling with the sponsorship of more and more "radical" ideas—he was one of those rather rare men who grow more radical with the advancing years—made him an embodiment of the finest characteristics and of the contradictions of the mid- and late-Victorian age.

Progressive Democratization of Britain. During the debate on the Second Reform Bill, John Stuart Mill (1806-1873), in many ways the foremost political thinker of his time, moved the enfranchisement of women. It is less important to note, that the motion was defeated than to state that seventy-eight members voted for it and 169 against it.* In February 1868 the conservative Prime Minister Lord Derby resigned. Disraeli became now for the first time the leader of the party and Prime Minister.

In the fall elections were held and the Liberals were swept into power. Gladstone's first concern was for Ireland. After the Fenian troubles, inspired by Irish Americans who founded the Fenian Brotherhood (named after the legendary armed force Fianna of ancient times), had died down by 1867, Gladstone worked for the conciliation of the Irish Catholic peasantry. The first step was the disestablishment of the (Anglican) Church of Ireland. Then Gladstone turned his attention to land reform, the improvement of the tenants' status. But the (first) Irish Land Act of 1870 did not go far enough. It provided only compensation for tenants in case of eviction and for improvements; it did not yet take care of the two fundamental problems: fixity of tenure and fair rents. An even more fundamental Irish demand ("repeal of the Union") was then hardly considered. It was at that time neither demanded by the Irish Catholic hierarchy nor by the mass of the Irish peasantry.

* Mill published in 1869 *The Subjection of Women,* which he had written in 1861. In the first paragraph he stated, "That the principle which regulates the existing social relations between the two sexes—the legal subordination of one sex to the other —is wrong in itself, and now one of the chief hindrances to human improvement; and that it ought to be replaced by a principle of perfect equality, admitting no power or privilege on the one side, nor disability on the other."

Of greater importance for English democracy were two other acts of 1870. The Education Act, sponsored by William Edward Forster (1818-1886), laid the foundations for compulsory and general elementary education. Locally elected school boards received the right to levy taxes and to build and to maintain non-denominational schools (the board schools), in which religion was not taught and which supplemented the existing church and private schools. At the same time all branches of the civil service, with the exception of the Foreign Office, were made accessible to all those who passed competitive examinations. In 1871 the ancient universities of Oxford and Cambridge were made accessible to men of all creeds on equal terms. The system of obtaining commission and promotion in the army was abolished, in spite of bitter resistance from many older officers, and thus the way for trained and competent leadership was opened. In 1872 voting was made secret (the Ballot Act), and this step made the formation of an independent Irish party possible, diminishing sharply the influence of the landlords, exercised in the former system of open voting.

Gladstone resigned in 1874, and the elections turned out in favor of the Conservatives under Disraeli, who meanwhile had broadened his party's appeal and strengthened its organization. (*See Reading No. 11.*) But Disraeli was now a sick and lonely elderly man, and the structure of his party-following did not allow him to carry through his plans for social reforms. Nevertheless, in the year 1875 a broadened Trade Union Act legalized peaceful picketing and collective bargaining; and an Artisans' Dwelling Act and a Public Health Act laid the foundations for future developments of social legislation. But beginning in 1876 Disraeli's and the country's attention turned to foreign and imperial affairs.

The Age of Imperialism. Though the zenith of American and European imperialism was reached in the 1890's, Disraeli became one of its early spokesmen. His interest in the East— which meant then the Near and Middle East, the road to India —had always been lively. In 1847 he published a novel *Tancred or The New Crusade*. Tancred goes to Palestine and Syria, and one of the Arabs there tells him: "You must . . . quit a petty and exhausted position for a vast and prolific empire. Let the

Queen of the English collect a great fleet, let her stow away all her treasure, bullion, gold plate, and precious arms; be accompanied by all her court and chief people, and transfer the seat of her empire from London to Delhi." Even thirty years later Disraeli declared *Tancred* his favorite work. By then, in 1876, he proposed to add "Empress of India" to the titles of his beloved Queen. One year before Disraeli acquired a very large number of shares of the French-directed Suez Canal Company, about seven-sixteenths of the whole capital, which had been held by the khedive Ismail who ruled Egypt from 1863 to 1879. Disraeli paid for the shares the sum of almost four million pound sterling, an investment which was not only financially most rewarding but prepared the British occupation of Egypt seven years later.

The most important chapter in Disraeli's career was, however, connected with the Balkan unrest of 1876, the Russian-Turkish war of 1877-78, and the Berlin Conference of 1878 which will be discussed later. At the Berlin Conference Disraeli not only succeeded in averting a war between Russia and Britain but in resettling the Balkan affairs in a way acceptable to Britain and its interest in preserving the Ottoman empire. Britain received the right to occupy and administer the Turkish island of Cyprus against the promise of maintaining the integrity of Turkey in Asia. At the Berlin Conference Disraeli was supported by his new foreign secretary, the third Marquess of Salisbury (1830-1903) who was to become his successor as leader of the conservative party. When Disraeli, who in 1876 had become Earl of Beaconsfield, returned from Berlin, he declared that he had brought home "peace with honor." That was Disraeli's last triumph. He was by that time a sick man, lonely after the death of his beloved wife (*see Reading No. 12*) but supported by his friendship with the Queen (*see Reading No. 13*).

When in 1876 the Turkish massacres in Bulgaria became known in Britain, Gladstone made himself the spokesman of the Christian Balkan population. In his pamphlet *The Bulgarian Horrors and the Question of the East* he sharply attacked the government's pro-Turkish policy. "Let the Turks now carry away their abuses in the only possible manner, namely by carrying off themselves," the pamphlet ended, ". . . one and all, bag and baggage, shall I hope clear out from the province they have desolated and profaned." Many of Britain's leading intellectuals sided with Gladstone, but after the outbreak of the war the people-at-large supported Disraeli and the word "jingoism" was added to the English language, taken from a famous music hall song then widely heard throughout Britain.

Gladstone's anti-imperialism gained wider influence by the troubles which befell British armies in South Africa in the war against the Zulus and in Afghanistan. The impact of Gladstone's campaign speeches—he was the first British statesman to "stump the country"—was heightened by the economic depression, produced among other factors by the influx of cheap food stuff from overseas. Many European countries introduced tariffs to protect their farmers. Disraeli clung to the free trade policy which thirty years before he had combated. This decision not only increased Britain's dependence on food from abroad, it aggravated also the situation of the Irish farmer and went a long way to acerbate the Irish crisis. When Beaconsfield dissolved the House, the elections in the early spring of 1880 brought in a large liberal majority. Gladstone became for the second time prime minister (1880-1885); but his party was disunited, especially on the issue now raised with greatest urgency, Irish home rule. It was only with hesitation that Gladstone undertook this difficult task. (*See Reading No. 14.*)

CHAPTER 7

Europe's Expansion

The last third of the nineteenth century was the period of the great expansion of European political, economic, and cultural influence. Members of the Asian and African elites were introduced in this period to the European tradition, partly in French or British universities and partly in schools maintained by missionary societies in their homelands. European concepts of public life and rational organization were implanted in the thinking of non-Europeans who, as a result, became reformers in their own societies. Books in European languages were translated into the native languages or read in their original, and with their help ideas like national self-determination and secularism began to exercise their influence. Though the traditional ways of thought and structure of society continued to prevail, the foundations for a Europeanization of the globe were laid.

The Europeanization of the Globe. In their *Communist Manifesto* Karl Marx and Friedrich Engels wrote, that

> In place of old local and national seclusion and self-sufficiency, we have intercourse in every direction, universal interdependence of nations, and as in material, so also in intellectual production. The intellectual creations of individual nations become common property. . . . The bourgeoisie, by the rapid improvement of all instruments of production, by the immensely facilitated means of communication, draws all, even the most barbarian nations, into civilization. . . . It compels all nations . . . to introduce what it calls civilization into their midst. . . . In one word, it creates a world after its own image.

Yet when Marx and Engels wrote these words in November 1847, the technological revolution was only in its beginning and many parts of the globe remained unknown and inaccessible. China and Japan were for all practical purposes still closed to European penetration. The spread of European civilization was, of course, primarily not a question of class. What Marx and Engels called "bourgeois" civilization might better be called industrial or modern society.

The superiority of Europe then was not only, and even not mainly, based on industrial, scientific, or technological developments but on a more efficient and less corrupt administration, on the equality of all citizens before the law, on at least theoretical recognition of the dignity of every individual, on the tolerance of dissent and opposition. Yet these achievements were reached in Europe, too, only recently, at the end of the seventeenth century in England and Holland. They spread then to the European continent in the age of Enlightenment, and to many parts of Europe much later. It was not a process confined to "darker" races. The process of Westernization which took place in Asia and Africa in the early twentieth century was similar to that which reached Russia in the eighteenth and the Balkans in the early nineteenth century. Westernization does not imply a difference of race or religion. In Africa, Ethiopa was an ancient Christian land, but it became subject to the process of Westernization only relatively late in the twentieth century.

Africa. The last great land mass to be subjected to this process of Westernization or the introduction of modern civilization which from the beginning was envisaged as a universal civilization was Africa, the "dark continent." Only by 1890 "the main features of the Nile basin," a riddle for more than two thousand years, became known. In this exploration Mehmed Emin Pasha (originally Eduard Schnitzer, 1840-1892), governor of the equatorial province of the Egyptian Sudan, played a great role. The interior of Africa was explored by the Scottish missionary David Livingstone (1813-1873) and the British journalist Sir Henry Morton Stanley (1841-1904), who was sent out by the *New York Herald* to find Livingstone from whom no news had reached the West in several years. Stanley found him in 1871. In 1855 Livingstone "for the first time apprehended the true form of the African river system and the continent" and later explored the Zambezi river and the Nyasa and Tanganyika lakes. His work was continued by Stanley who traced the whole course of the Congo river. It was primarily due to him that King Leopold II of Belgium (1835-1909) organized an international conference in Brussels in 1876 for the exploration and exploitation of the newly discovered interior of Africa, especially of the Congo basin.

The Far East. Africa was then believed to be a continent of primitive tribes without history or civilization. Different, of course, was the situation in China and Japan, countries of very ancient and highly developed civilizations and societal organization, which in many respects were superior to that of medieval Europe. These countries were opened up to European and American cultural and commercial penetration only in the second third of the nineteenth century. The attitude of the elites of these two Far Eastern countries to the challenge of Westernization was very different. The Chinese, conscious of the greatness of their civilization so much older than Europe's and of their imperial position as the "Middle Kingdom," the heart of the terrestrial and celestial order, refused in the nineteenth century to compromise with the alien and "inferior" civilization of the West. This attitude brought upon them a century of profound humiliation. In 1842 China was defeated by Britain, and in 1844 Caleb Cushing (1800-1879) negotiated on behalf of the United States a treaty with China which became the model for all future "unequal" treaties. It placed all Americans in China under the extraterritorial jurisdiction of their consuls or mixed tribunals. The legal toleration of Roman Catholicism was imposed upon China in 1844 and that of Protestants the following year.

The Taiping Rebellion in central China further weakened the imperial regime. The rebellion which lasted from 1850 to 1864 was directed against the Manchu dynasty and had nationalist, social, and religious aspects. It was suppressed by the "ever victorious army," commanded by the British officer Charles George Gordon (1833-1885), who was later to play a great role in Egyptian services in the Sudan. During the rebellion Great Britain, France, the United States, and Russia forced China in the treaties of Tientsin not only to open more ports but to permit the establishment of foreign legations in Peking and the penetration of Christian missionaries into the interior of China. China's maritime customs were put under foreign inspectors, and the importation of opium was legalized. Two years later British and French troops occupied Peking and burned the summer palace, recalling to the Chinese the conduct of former barbarian invaders.

During the same period France established her control over Indochina, first in the southern part, called then Cochin-China. Saigon was occupied in 1859; and the three eastern provinces of

Cochin-China were ceded to France in 1862, and the three western provinces were annexed in 1867 to what had become a
French colony governed then by the French navy. A French
protectorate over Annam in the central part and over Tongking
in the north of what is today called Vietnam, was after much
struggle established in 1883. Yet the country was long plagued
by nationalist rebellions, generally called by the French banditry.

As Indochina south of China was opened up and subjected by
the French, so the secluded kingdom of Korea to the northeast
of China was in the 1870's opened up by American and Japanese
pressure. The first attempt of an American naval force to land
marines in 1871 was unsuccessful. In 1876 Japan was more
successful in concluding a treaty with Korea, which opened three
ports to outside trade. Finally in 1882 the United States secured
extra-territorial rights for its citizens and permission to trade in
the Kingdom, and similar treaties with other powers followed
in quick succession.

Japan's Modernization. By 1876, when Japan acted in
Korea, she was on the road to Westernization. In an early stage
of her contacts with the West, Japan decided to accept those
aspects of Western civilization which her leaders believed necessary to their survival in the new world, which suddenly demanded
entrance into Japan's secluded and isolationist existence. After
Commodore Matthew Galbraith Perry (1794-1858) visited
the Bay of Yedo with an American squadron in July 1853 and
returned in February 1854, he concluded on March 31, 1854, a
treaty with the Japanese which opened two Japanese ports to
American vessels. From that time on foreigners began to settle
in Japanese coastal ports. Violent struggles in Japan followed
about the problem how to meet this intrusion of foreign elements.
Bombardments and naval demonstrations by American, British,
Dutch, and French forces were intertwined with domestic civil
wars. In 1868 the young emperor Mutsuhito (1852-1912), the
122nd in direct lineage from the legendary founder of the dynasty
in 660 B.C., who resided in Kyoto, the imperial residence since
794, became the head of the faction seeking thorough reforms.
The forces of the shogun, the military regent residing in Yedo,
were defeated and the emperor's residence transferred to Yedo,
renamed Tokyo. The era of reforms, called Meiji (enlightened

peace), thus started under the most traditional and strictly national leadership. Step by step the ancient feudal order was replaced by a modern bureaucratic administration, and modern industry transformed Japan's economy. Religious tolerance and the Georgian calender were introduced in 1873, and Japan was set on the road of becoming a major modern power. She could abolish in 1899 the unequal treaties, imposed upon her in the 1850's and 1860's. The first Western country to agree to the recognition of Japan's equality with the West was Britain.

Russia's Expansion in Asia. In the 1860's Russia was the first European country to expand into the northern Far East and into the heart of central Asia. After her defeat in the Crimean war (1855), Russia turned eastward. At that time she was represented by the brilliant Count Nicholas Muravyev-Amursky (1810-1889) as governor-general of eastern Siberia (1842-1862). In 1858 and in 1860 he acquired from China parts of Manchuria north of the Amur river and then the coastal province between the Ussuri river, a tributary of the Amur, and the Pacific Ocean. There Russia founded the city of Khabarovsk at the confluence of the Amur and the Ussuri rivers, and the port of Vladivostok, a name which means ruler of the East. But even Vladivostok was not an ice-free port in winter, and a few decades later Russia tried to push southward to gain such a port. But between 1865 and 1882 she directed her attention to central Asia, a country of Mohammedan principalities and populations, most of them speaking Turkish dialects and therefore called Turkestan.

The conquest began with the capture of Tashkent by General Mikhail Cherniayev (1828-1889). The two Islamic principalities of Bukhara and Khiva became Russian dependencies, whereas Fergana on the frontier of Chinese Turkestan (Sin-Kiang) came like Tashkent under direct Russian rule. The same happened after the conquest of Turkmenistan in the western part of Turkestan. The Russians took in 1881 the Turkoman fortress of Geok-Tepe and the most ancient oasis of Merv in 1883. Thus Russia became the immediate neighbor of Persia and Afghanistan which formed from then on buffer states between Asiatic Russia and British India. In the east the two countries were separated only by a very narrow though extremely mountainous strip. The British resented this Russian advance as a threat to their position in India and on the Persian Gulf, which guarded the western approaches to India. A clash between Russia and Britain for the control of Asia seemed imminent. The goal of this struggle was the control of India.

India. In the eighteenth century the British emerged victorious from the imperialist struggle among themselves, the French, the Dutch, and the Portuguese, for the control of the Indian subcontinent. In the same war (1756-1763) in which the British put an end to French rule in Canada, the battle of Plassey (1757) in west Bengal, where the British fought under the command of Robert Clive (1725-1774), decided the fate of India. The country was then officially still under the rule of the Mohammedan Great Mogul in Delhi, a rule established in 1526. The vast subcontinent had never been unified as a whole by any native prince or foreign conqueror. The British succeeded in this task in the nineteenth century. Originally they administered the territories then under their rule through the British East India Company, a private trading company whose charter dated from the reign of Queen Elizabeth I (1600).

In 1857 a revolt of the native armed forces of the Company led to the perpetration of great cruelty on both sides, the traumatic memory of which resulted in a long-lasting distrust and antagonism of the two races. One of the consequences of the mutiny was the termination of the rule of the company and of the by then nominal rule of the Mogul dynasty. India became a British Crown Colony, except for the many native states whose princes entered into treaty relationship with the British Crown. A proclamation of Queen Victoria (*see Reading No. 15*) promised equality of all races. On January 1, 1877, Queen Victoria assumed the title of Empress of India, and India was for seventy years the "jewel" of the British Crown (*see Reading No. 16*). India played in modern Asia a role similar to that of Italy in the Mediterranean of antiquity. India found herself in a central position in Asia between Islamic West Asia and the Hindu and Buddhist East Asia and participated in both of these civilizations. Through the early awakening of an enlightened native leadership and the early maturity of Indian nationalism—both thanks to British liberalism—India played a great role in the Westernization of Asia. Only half a century after becoming a Crown Colony, the Indian elite organized since 1885 in the Indian National Congress demanded internal self-government or dominion status, as it had been achieved before 1914 by the British inhabited colonies. The first of them was Canada, where the first Earl of Durham (1792-1840) suggested in his report of 1839 the introduction of domestic self-government. His son-in-law, the eighth Lord Elgin (1811-1863), instituted less than a decade later a fully parliamentary regime with the responsibility of the Canadian ministers to the elected colonial legislature. In 1867 the British North American Act applied the principle of federalism to the various North American colonies which (with the exception of Newfoundland) were united into the Dominion of Canada. By 1869 the Dominion extended from the Atlantic to the Pacific Ocean and a short time later railroads connected and opened up the vast and only sparely inhabited regions of the Canadian west with the Canadian east. The Canadian example was later followed by the Commonwealth of Australia and the Dominion of New Zealand, but it proved much more difficult to apply the principle of dominion status to parts of the empire which were not inhabited by settlers of British descent, like Ireland and the Union of South Africa.

The Suez Canal. It was in the second third of the nineteenth century that West and East were connected by a water way which shortened the distance between them considerably and realized a dream going back to ancient times. A French engineer, Ferdinand de Lesseps (1805-1894) who had spent several years as a consul in Egypt, conceived the plan in 1832; and in 1854 he received the concession to build such a canal from Said Pasha, Viceroy of Egypt (1854-1863). De Lesseps founded the Compagnie Universelle du Canal Maritime de Suez as a French joint-stock company with 400,000 shares of five hundred gold francs each. French investors took up 207,111 of these shares; a small number was subscribed by others, especially Belgians, and the Egyptian government had to accept the rest of the shares, numbering 177,642. As was pointed out (see p. 59) the British government acquired in 1875 these shares held by the Egyptian government and thus became a large minority owner of the Compagnie which was established under French law with its seat in Paris. Thus Britain entered decisively into an enterprise which she and the United States had originally refused to participate in.

Said who died in 1863 was followed as Egyptian viceroy or khedive by his nephew Ismail (lived 1830-1895, ruled 1863-1879). It was during his reign that the building of the Suez Canal which started in 1859 was finished in 1869. On November 17 of that year the Canal, a 100-mile-long waterway from Port Said in the Mediterranean to Suez on the Red Sea, was officially opened with great pomp and the participation of representatives of the European ruling houses. The Italian operatic composer Giuseppe Verdi (1813-1901) wrote his opera *Aida* for that occasion, but it was only performed in 1871 in the Royal Opera house which Ismail built in Cairo.

Though the cost of construction of the Canal was very high, the Company has earned steadily increasing surpluses since 1872. In the nineteenth century no other artificial waterway approached the Suez Canal in importance to world trade and world communications. It made the greatest revolution in transit by sea since the discovery of the sea routes to America and India. It helped the steamship to its final victory over the sailing ship. In the Red Sea with its frequent calms, the sailing ship was at a hopeless disadvantage; while on the long route around the west coast of Africa, with its few harbors, the steamship had proved less serviceable. The Suez Canal brought the British possessions in India into the mainstream of world trade and revived the importance of the European Mediterranean ports. The passage from London to Bombay via Suez is 4881 nautical miles shorter than the passage around the Cape; the saving from Hamburg is much the same, and the saving from Marseilles and Trieste is even greater. In 1870 486 vessels passed the Canal; by 1913 the figure had risen to 5085 vessels. During the whole period ships of Great Britain were leading in the Canal traffic in numbers and tonnage. Lord Curzon of Kedleston (1859-1925), who was Viceroy of India from 1899 to 1905, declared in 1909 in a lecture in Edinburgh on "The Place of India in the Empire":

> Consider in the first place what a part India has played in the shaping of British policy and the expansion of the British dominion. It has been the determining influence in every con-

siderable movement of British power to the east and south of the Mediterranean. The Eastern question of the Middle Ages was merely the recovery of the Holy Places from infidel hands. But once we had planted ourselves in India, the Eastern question, though it revolved round Constantinople, was in reality directed by considerations of the security of our Indian possessions. But for India, Lord Beaconsfield would not have bought the shares in the Suez Canal; and but for the Suez Canal, we should not now be in Egypt. The historic rivalry and struggles with Russia for nearly a century sprang from the supposed necessity of keeping her far away from the frontiers of India. (*See Reading No. 16.*)

CHAPTER 8

The Eastern Question

In the second third of the nineteenth century the Eastern question continued to be what is called today the Near or Middle Eastern question. The period discussed in this volume started with the Eastern question and a Russian-Turkish war in 1853, the Crimean War; it ends with another flare-up of the Eastern question and another Russian-Turkish war twenty-five years later. At the end of the Crimean War, the Turkish government promised in the Hatt-i-Humayoun important reforms for the non-Islamic populations of the empire (*see Reading No. 17*), and in the Treaty of Paris (March 30, 1856) Turkey was admitted to the European concert. Though there followed a Westernization of Turkish literature and of the education of the Turkish elite, the Turkish government itself did not become liberal. Thus the failure of the reform movement disappointed the Christian Balkan peoples who, under European influence, soon did not demand mere reforms but full independence. The aspirations of these Greek Orthodox, and in their majority Slavic peoples, were supported by Russia, the leading Greek Orthodox and Slavic power.

Pan-Slavism. Pan-Slavism, a movement for the close co-operation and ultimately political union of all Slav-speaking peoples, the majority of which lived then in the Ottoman and Habsburg empires, was first developed in Austria as a protection against Germanization and Magyarization. In 1848 a Pan-Slav congress held in Prague (in Austrian Bohemia, which after 1918 became the capital of Czechoslovakia) tried to organize the aspirations of the Slav peoples in the Habsburg monarchy for equality and federalism. The achievement of Italian and German unification in the 1860's stimulated the rise of Pan-Slavism in Russia as a way of expanding Russian influence to the Balkans and to the Danube basin. The Austro-Hungarian Compromise of 1867 turned the hopes of the disappointed Austrian Slavs towards Russia. A second Pan-Slav conference was held in

Moscow in 1867; and the leaders of the Czech national movement, František Palacký (1798-1876) and his son-in-law Ladislav Rieger (1818-1903), attended the Moscow conference. But the Poles and the Ukrainians, both feeling oppressed by the Russians, remained aloof. The Polish uprising of 1863 strengthened Russian nationalism and the Russian imperialist character of the new Pan-Slav movement. Nicholas Danilevsky (1822-1885) published in his book *Russia and Europe, an Inquiry into the Cultural and Political Relations of the Slav to the German-Latin World* (1869) a summing-up of the Pan-Slav ideology of the time. (*See Reading No. 18.*) Nicolas Ignatiev (1832-1908), who served as Russian ambassador at Constantinople from 1864 to 1877, was a convinced Pan-Slav. Thus Russia in the 1870's supported, as did Gladstone for other reasons, the uprisings and "wars of national liberation," which the Balkan Slavs fought against the Turks.

Unrest among the Christians.   Ottoman rule, which started in the Balkans in the fourteenth century, had been for the Christian populations on the whole a beneficial rule compared with that of the local Slav or Rumanian nobility, the Boyars. The condition of the peasantry improved; military service was not exacted from the Christians; and no systematic effort was made to convert them or to suppress their native languages. This lasted until the early eighteenth century when the Ottoman power began to dwindle and Russia and Austria began to compete for influence among the Balkan Christians. From that time on the Christian provinces of the Ottoman empire were plagued by frequent insurrections, often · suppressed by the Turks with great severity. One of the provinces where frequent insurrections happened was Bosnia-Herzegovina, inhabited by a population speaking the Serbo-Croatian language but divided into three religious groups—Mohammedan, Greek Orthodox, and Roman Catholic. Bosnia-Herzegovina was located in the northwestern part of the Balkans and separated Serbia from Croatian-speaking Dalmatia and from access to the Adriatic Sea.

The chief European powers, interested in the uprising in Bosnia-Herzegovina, were Russia with its Pan-Slav ideology, Austria-Hungary which wished to prevent the formation on its southern border of a Great Serbia as the "Piedmont" of a future southern Slav unity, and Germany where Bismarck intended to compensate the Habsburgs for the loss of their dominant position in Germany by an expansion into the Balkans. In addition, the British government, then under Disraeli's leadership, feared Russia's advance toward Constantinople and the Straits. This British policy sprang "from the natural suggestions of self-defence against the march of a dangerous rivalry. It was backed by the consenting instinct of the people." This policy saw "in Russia a power which unless firmly kept within bounds, would dominate Europe; more particularly that it would undermine and supersede British policy in the East." Disraeli and many British statesmen thought it a duty "to contrive that Great Britain should be subject to Russian ascendancy (if ever), at the remotest period allowed by destiny." * Thus a policy of the containment of Russia developed.

The Bulgarian Uprising. Of all the southern Slav peoples the Bulgarians were least known in Europe. Their national revival came later than that of the Serbians, Greeks, or Rumanians. The first goal in their struggle for national identity was directed against the Greek Orthodox priesthood, imposed upon them by the Greek Orthodox Patriarch of Constantinople. The few existing schools were then conducted in Greek; and the Bulgarian language, a Slav language, was written in Greek characters. Finally the Bulgarians succeeded in 1870 in establishing an independent Bulgarian Orthodox exarchate and began to develop their own literature, a mighty stimulant to the national awakening of this peasant people. In May 1876 they rose against the Turks and massacred many Turkish officials, which brought about Turkish vengeance, the "Bulgarian atrocities" which aroused Gladstone's fury (see p. 59).

The Serbian-Turkish War. This unrest served as a pretense for the Serbs who, on June 30, 1876, under Prince Milan I of the House of Obrenović (1868-1889), trusting in Russian support

---

* *The Encyclopaedia Britannica,* 11th printing (1910), Vol. III, p. 569. As we saw, many British statesmen under Gladstone opposed this policy. Disraeli could not foresee that for the next ninety years there would be no Anglo-Russian war, but Anglo-Russian co-operation in two wars against Germany and that in the secret treaty of 1915 Britain would agree to the occupation of Constantinople by the Russians.

and hoping for the acquisition of Bosnia-Herzegovina, declared war on Turkey. In spite of the fact that the independent Serbian-speaking principality of Montenegro under Prince Nicholas I (1860-1918) joined Serbia and that these Balkan Slavs were fighting with the help of a great number of Russian volunteers acting under the inspiration of Pan-Slavism, and that the army was commanded by the Russian general Cherniayev, the victor of Tashkent (see p. 65), the Serbian army was decisively defeated by the Turks and only a Russian ultimatum saved her national existence. Meanwhile, on July 8, 1876, Russia and Austria-Hungary concluded an agreement in Reichstadt in northern Bohemia which promised Bessarabia to Russia and Bosnia-Herzegovina to Austria-Hungary and established general principles for the reform and distribution of Ottoman lands. Similar, though with different details, demands for reform of the Ottoman empire were raised at the Constantinople Conference between Britain and Russia in December 1876.

All these demands came to nothing when Abdul Hamid II (1876-1909) became Sultan of the Ottoman empire and the grand vizier or prime minister Midhat Pasha (1822-1884), a liberal reformer, proclaimed on December 23, 1876, a liberal constitution which guaranteed on the one hand the rights of the individual, on the other hand the indivisibility of the Ottoman empire where the non-Islamic population was to be integrated on the footing of complete equality into a new Ottoman nationality. Though a first Ottoman parliament met on March 19, 1877, and tried to put the reforms on a legal basis, this episode of the early Westernization of the empire was short-lived. Abdul Hamid dismissed Midhat Pasha, prorogued the parliament, suspended the constitution, and ruled as an autocrat until 1908 when a group of officers (the Young Turks) took up the reforms started by Midhat Pasha.

The Russo-Turkish War. The Pan-Slav enthusiasm in Russia forced Emperor Alexander II to declare war on Turkey in April 1877. The Russian armies, supported by the Rumanians, had great difficulty crossing the Balkan mountains. Their siege of Plevna in northern Bulgaria lasted for 143 days. Only after the fall of Plevna in December could the Russians advance toward Constantinople. They stopped short of a siege of the

city, in view of the fact that the British government sent a fleet
to Constantinople and had Indian soldiers moved to Malta. The
treaty of San Stefano of March 1878 between Russia and Turkey
created a large Bulgaria, which included most of Macedonia and
an access to the Aegean Sea. On the Caucasian front the
victorious Russians received Ardahan and Kars in northeastern
Anatolia and Batum on the eastern shores of the Black Sea from
Turkey.*

The creation of a great Bulgaria which was then considered a
Russian satellite with a potential naval base in the Aegean which
could be used by Russia and give her the long desired access to
warm and open seas, aroused the opposition of Britain. The
Great Bulgaria created at San Stefano constituted three-fifths of
the Balkan Peninsula. It evoked not only the suspicion of some
European powers but also the hostility of the Serbs. The Serbs
were, like the Bulgarians, a Slav-speaking people of the Greek
Orthodox faith, and for centuries subject to Turkish rule. Yet
reminiscences from the Middle Ages recalled to both peoples
their competition for hegemony in the Balkan Peninsula and for
the control of Macedonia. In fact, from the time of the liberation of the two peoples from Turkish domination, the two
closely related nations of Serbs and Bulgarians were frequently
at war against each other and found themselves on opposite
sides in the two world wars of the twentieth century.

The Berlin Congress. Upon the initiative of Count Andrássy, the foreign minister of Austria-Hungary, Bismarck called
upon the six European Great Powers and Turkey to meet in
Berlin and to settle the Eastern question. The Congress assembled on June 13, 1878, and ended one month later by a
treaty which replaced the treaty of San Stefano. The new treaty
declared the principalities of Rumania, Serbia, and Montenegro
fully independent and sovereign states, ending thereby the
suzerainty of Turkey. The two last named principalities received
territorial aggrandizements. In 1881 the Prince of Rumania proclaimed himself King. He followed a pro-Austrian policy and
concluded in 1883 a secret alliance with Austria, dictated by

* Ardahan and Kars were returned to Turkey by Soviet Russia in
    1921. Batum on the Black Sea forms the terminus of the oil
    pipe line from Baku on the Caspian Sea.

the fear of Russia. This fear was based, among other factors, on the fact that at the Berlin Congress Rumania had to cede Bessarabia to Russia in exchange for the Bulgarian Dobruja south of the mouth of the Danube. Yet the pro-Austrian policy was not popular with the majority of the Rumanian people who complained that Transylvania, inhabited by a large number of Rumanian peasants, was under Hungarian domination without any consideration for the rights of this numerous minority. Similarly, the pro-Austrian policy of Prince Milan of Serbia was not popular with the Serbian people. It was opposed above all by the Russophile Radical Party under Nicholas Pašić (1846-1926). Prince Milan, too, assumed the title of King of Serbia in 1882.*

The main outcome of the Berlin Congress concerned Bulgaria. Instead of the Great Bulgaria envisaged in the treaty of San Stefano a very small Bulgaria was created between the Danube and the Balkan mountains as a principality under Turkish suzerainty. The Bulgarians, a peasant people without a native aristocracy, drew up a democratic constitution at Trnovo, the ancient capital of Bulgaria, which was replaced in 1879 by Sofia, its present capital. In Trnovo the Bulgarian notables elected Prince Alexander of Battenberg (1857-1893) as their ruler. He was a descendant of the ruling house of the German grand duchy of Hesse and the nephew of the Russian emperor. He had participated in the Russian-Turkish war which liberated Bulgaria.†

The part of Bulgaria, south of the Balkan mountains, with the capital of Plovdiv (Philippopolis) was constituted as an autonomous Turkish province, Eastern Rumelia, under a Christian governor. The separation of the two Bulgarias did not last long. In 1885 the Rumelians proclaimed their union with Bulgaria,

---

* Milan abdicated in 1889 after a victory of the Radical Party and was followed by his son Alexander who ruled from 1889 to 1903. The Prince of Montenegro proclaimed himself King only in 1910.

† In 1917 the English members of the house of Battenberg changed their name to Mountbatten. One of them, Louis (b. 1900), led the campaign recapturing Burma from Japan and was the last British viceroy of India; another, Prince Philip (b. 1921) became the husband of Queen Elizabeth II.

a step which angered Serbia as disturbing the balance in the Balkans. A Serbo-Bulgarian war followed in which the Serbs were defeated at Slivnica, west of Sofia, and the status quo was restored. Alexander was proclaimed Prince of Bulgaria and Governor General of Eastern Rumelia, but Russia's discontent with Alexander led to his capture by a conspiracy of pro-Russian officers and his exile from Bulgaria. After a lengthy search for a new ruler, Prince Ferdinand of Saxe-Coburg-Gotha (1861-1948) became Prince of Bulgaria and Governor General of Eastern Rumelia. In 1908 he assumed the title of King (Tsar) of an officially unified, independent, and sovereign Bulgaria.

These decisions of the Congress of Berlin left Macedonia, with its mixed population, speaking Bulgarian, Greek, and Serbian local dialects for three more decades under Turkish rule. But even to the present day, after several armed conflicts, Macedonia has remained a subject of contention, primarily between Serbia and Bulgaria. The former have been victorious, both in the second Balkan war (1913) and in the two world wars. But Greece had an interest there, too. At the Congress of Berlin she was promised Thessaly and part of Epirus, which she finally gained by a convention with Turkey in 1881. But when Greece, as a result of the events in Eastern Rumelia in 1885, tried to extend her territory, especially by the annexation of the island of Crete, she was unsuccessful. In fact, in a war with Turkey in 1896/97 in which Greece supported one of the several Cretan insurrections, Greece was decisively defeated. Only the inter-vention of the European powers saved her from paying for her defeat and deprived Turkey of the fruits of her victory.

Another island, inhabited by a majority of Greek-speaking Orthodox Christians but geographically remote from Greece and much nearer to the Turkish coast, was Cyprus. The island was under Turkish domination from 1571 on, when the Turks ex-pelled the Venetians. At the time of the Congress of Berlin, Turkey agreed to put the island of Cyprus under British adminis-tration against the British promise to defend the position of Turkey in Asia. Turkish sovereignty was recognized; but in 1914, when Turkey entered the war against Britain as an ally of Germany, Cyprus became part of the British empire.

The most fateful decision of the Congress of Berlin, however, was found in Article 25. It put the Turkish provinces of Bosnia and Herzegovina under the occupation and administration of Austria-Hungary. The population, especially its Greek Orthodox and Mohammedan parts, resisted the occupation and the Austro-Hungarian army had to fight for several months to make the claims of the Habsburg monarchy valid. The administration of Bosnia-Herzegovina was, as was that of Alsace-Lorraine, a direct responsibility of the whole monarchy and was placed under the supervision of the common Austro-Hungarian minister of finance. The Turkish *sanjak* (district) of Novi Bazar, which extends in a southeasterly direction from Herzegovina and separates Serbia from Montenegro, though forming part of the Turkish vilayet (province) of Bosnia, was left under Turkish administration. But the Austro-Hungarian monarchy received the right of keeping garrisons and of building and maintaining military and commercial roads there. When in 1908 Austria-Hungary annexed Bosnia-Herzegovina, she abandoned her rights in Novi Bazar and the territory was divided between Serbia and Montenegro in the Balkan wars (1912-13). This expansion of the Dual Monarchy into the Balkans under Count Julius Andrássy as foreign minister was, in its consequences for European peace, as unfortunate as the annexation by Germany of Alsace-Lorraine. Both annexations were carried through against the will of the population and can be regarded as the immediate causes for the outbreak of the Great War of 1914. Long before that event, they threw their shadow on European international relations which led after a deceptive era of peace to the catastrophe of 1914. Bismarck's attempt to contain France through a system of alliances proved futile.

CHAPTER 9

The System of Alliances

East against West. The Holy Alliance of the three conservative and military empires of the East which existed after 1815—Russia, Austria-Hungary, and Prussia-Germany—was revived by Bismarck after 1870 in his effort to maintain French isolation after her defeat and thus to protect Germany from a war of revenge. However, Bismarck's fears were not based only on French desire to regain Alsace-Lorraine. He was even more worried lest Western democracy and republicanism endanger the survival of the conservative monarchies. Bismarck thought more in ideological, anti-democratic, and anti-republican terms than in nationalistic concepts which expressed themselves either in the wish of uniting all Germans in one Reich (Pan-Germanism) or of uniting all Slavs under Russian hegemony (Pan-Slavism). As Bismarck wrote himself in his *Gedanken und Erinnerungen:*

> If the monarchical governments (of the East) do not understand the necessity for uniting in the interest of the political and social order, but, on the contrary, become subservient to the chauvinistic impulses of their subjects, I fear that the international revolutionary and social conflicts which must be fought out, will be all the more dangerous, and will take on a character which will make the triumph of the monarchical order all the more difficult. Since 1871 I have sought for the most precise assurance against those conflicts in the alliance of the three (Eastern) emperors as well as in the effort to give the monarchical principle in Italy firm support by that alliance.

The Three Emperors' League. Following this line of thought, the three emperors of Russia, Germany, and Austria-Hungary met in Berlin in 1872; and the following year witnessed visits of the German Emperor in St. Petersburg, of the Italian King in Berlin, and of the Russian Emperor in Austria. But soon the Pan-German aspirations in Germany and the Pan-Slav trends in Russia grew stronger than Bismarck, who had used German nationalism as an instrument for Prussia's attainment of hegemony in Germany and in Europe, had expected. The time of dynastic wars or friendships as a foundation of international European politics was fast passing. As the last third of the nineteenth century opened, nationalism in its more extreme forms—no longer a means used for carrying out government policies but a force influencing them—asserted itself. At the Congress of Berlin the Russian Prince Alexander Gorchakov (1798-1883), who was since 1856 Russian foreign minister, was Russia's chief representative. Originally Gorchakov had supported Prussia against Austria and France, and his attitude had made the Prussian victory of 1866 and 1870 possible. Gorchakov expected in return diplomatic support from Bismarck. He got it in 1870/71 when Russia undid the Black Sea clauses of the treaty of Paris (1856) which locked the Russian Black Sea fleet within that sea. But he did not receive the same support in the Russian-Turkish war of 1877 and at the Congress of Berlin.

Though Bismarck claimed at the Congress of Berlin to act as "the honest broker" and though Russia regained the part of Bessarabia, which she had lost in the Crimean war, she had to make great concessions to Britain and to Austria-Hungary, which the Russian nationalists resented. After the death of Alexander II, his son and successor Alexander III, who ruled from 1881 to 1894, was regarded as strongly influenced by Russian nationalism and as rather anti-German. Gorchakov's successor as foreign minister, Nicholas de Giers (1820-1895), a Protestant of German origin, followed a pacific policy, though it was under him that the Franco-Russian rapprochement was effected. This rapprochement was a response to Bismarck's alliance treaty with Austria-Hungary.

The Dual Alliance of 1879. On October 7, 1879, Germany and Austria-Hungary signed in Vienna their treaty of alliance which remained in force until the end of the two empires. The first article of the secret treaty read: "Should contrary to their hope, and against the loyal desire of the two high contracting parties, one of the two empires be attacked by Russia, the high contracting parties are bound to come to the assistance, one of the other, with the whole war strength of their empires, and accordingly to conclude peace only together and upon mutual agreement." In case of aggression by another power against one of the contracting parties (what was meant, was French aggression against Germany) the other contracting party will observe a benevolent neutrality, except in case that the aggressor is supported by Russia, in which case the alliance prescribed in the first article would become operative. The alliance of Austria-Hungary with Germany was the crowning, though unfortunate, achievement of the Austro-Hungarian foreign minister Count Julius Andrássy. It fitted well into his generally anti-Russian and anti-Slav attitude. The Slavic peoples of the Habsburg monarchy in their majority did not welcome the alliance with Germany. They would have preferred, if an alliance were desirable at all, one with France. Only the Austrian Germans and the Magyars supported the dual alliance. Once the alliance was concluded, Count Andrássy resigned.

Prince Bismarck himself discussed in his *Gedanken und Errinnerungen* the reasons which moved him to conclude the alliance with Austria. (*See Reading No. 19.*) He was in no way blind to the weakness of the Habsburg monarchy, which was caused by the bitter conflicts of its various nationalities, above all in Bohemia. But he was afraid that Austria-Hungary might seek an entente with France and Britain and that, as a result, Germany might become isolated. He clung to the hope of renewing the three emperors' league, and succeeded in having a secret treaty with that intention signed in Berlin on June 18, 1881, and renewed in 1884. In 1887, when the three-emperors'-league treaty expired and Russia refused to sign another treaty with Austria-Hungary, Bismarck signed without Austria's knowledge a three years' secret treaty with Russia called the "reinsurance treaty." This treaty was not renewed by Germany after Bismarck's dismissal in March 1890; but as long as Bismarck was in office, he successfully followed a rather tenuous and secretive policy of alliances in order to keep France isolated.

The Triple Alliance of 1882.   Bismarck was eager to draw Italy into this system of alliances. It was not easy because Italy looked upon the Italian-speaking parts of the Habsburg monarchy, even upon those inhabited by a large majority of southern Slavs, like Dalmatia, as "unredeemed" (*irredenta*) lands waiting to be redeemed by inclusion into the new Italian kingdom.

Outwardly the relations between Italy and Austria-Hungary were correct. In 1873 King Victor Emmanuel II visited Francis Joseph in Vienna, eager to make certain that Austria would not actively support the papal claims to the restoration of the papal Roman territory annexed by Italy in 1870. In 1875 Francis Joseph met the Italian King in Venice, which less than ten years before had been Austrian territory. As a faithful Catholic, Francis Joseph could not pay an official visit to the Italian King in Rome because such a step would have aroused the bitter opposition of Pope Pius IX, who never forgot or forgave the spoliation of his temporal power by Victor Emmanuel.

In 1881 the Italian government, whose majority feared the French, favored closer ties with Germany. There were three reasons for it. Italy was financially and politically very weak and the regime was fundamentally unstable, threatened both by clerical and by republican opposition. Germany in its apparent strength promised solid support for the shaky Italian monarchy. The second reason was the existence of powerful Catholic clerical influences in France which took the side of the Pope in his resistance against the Italian kingdom and his desire of restoring the Papal state. Finally, and perhaps most important, France thwarted Italy's aspiration of annexing Tunisia where most of the European residents were of Italian descent. Tunisia was the seat of ancient Carthage, and sentimental images of Roman grandeur seemed to direct Italian imperial ambitions toward Tunisia. Thus Italy was shocked when the French, as compensation for Britain's acquisition of Cyprus at the Congress of Berlin, established, with British connivance, the protectorate over Tunisia in the treaty of Bardo on May 12, 1881.

In that situation the Italians turned to Germany. The new Italian King Humbert I (1844-1900), who followed his father Victor Emmanuel in 1878, visited Vienna in October 1881; and on May 20, 1882, the secret triple-alliance treaty between Germany, Austria-Hungary, and Italy was signed. It assured Germany of Italy's neutrality in case of a war with France. But Bismarck was even more eager to establish the alliance in order "to protect the Italian monarchy from the dangers which must inevitably arise from an alliance by treaty with France and from the reciprocal support of the radical elements of France and

Italy." The treaty, however, was never popular in Italy and proved its worthlessness in 1914. The irredentist movement against Austria-Hungary went on; and after the death of Pius IX in 1878, his successor Leo XIII (Gioacchino Pecci, 1810-1903) represented a more moderate policy, though he, too, regarded himself as "imprisoned" in the Vatican.

But even Bismarck's and Andrássy's original system of an Austro-German alliance was ultimately self-defeating. It led in the early 1890's to the formation of an opposite dual alliance between France and Russia and in the first decade of the twentieth century to Great Britain's abandonment of her policy of isolationism. Feeling threatened by Germany, though not by Austria-Hungary, Britain established an Entente with France and later with Russia. French statesmen had regarded the existence of the Habsburg monarchy as a counterweight to German expansion and as an essential element in the preservation of the balance of power in Europe. As Germany's partner, however, Austria-Hungary was drawn into the European power struggle in the wake of Germany's victory over France. The atmosphere in Europe grew more and more tense. The system of alliances made it difficult to localize a war in Europe. An originally local conflict threatened to develop into a general war. The preparations for such an eventuality, the increased budgets for the armed forces and the improvement of military technology, turned the last third of the European century into an era of a self-assured imperialism, opposed only, though ineffectively, by the growth of international socialism.

The Great Debate. By 1880 Europe was still feeling itself as a unit (the Berlin Congress was an instance of the Great Powers acting together) and as the masters of the world. But the unity of the Europe of the first third of the century had been undermined by Mazzini and destroyed by Cavour and Bismarck. In vain the Swiss conservative Catholic statesman Philip Anton von Segesser (1817-1888) of Lucerne had warned Bismarck. "The German hegemony will be of short duration," he wrote. "Surrounded by civilized people whom they can neither assimilate nor annihilate, the Germans have based their dominion on the idea of the absolute state, which threatens human liberty in its most inalienable concerns. . . . Prussia will assimilate the whole of Germany. The superiority of Prussia's organization, the strictly ordered spirit of its people, the high intelligence of its leadership which in every branch of public life guarantees effective unity and force, will bring about the complete unification of Germany. . . . One may rightly doubt whether this means a guarantee for the peace and civilization of Europe. . . . The principle of force, upon which this new formation in the centre of Europe has been built, cannot but go on developing according to its nature." *

Leading spokesmen of Britain and France upheld the idea of a united liberal Europe based upon a "new law of nations . . . a moral empire," founded upon the "confidence of several peoples, not upon their fears, their passions, or their antipathies" (See Reading No. 20), and warned the Germans that their expansion westwards excused by historical and ethnic rights might be followed by a similar expansion of the Slavs, but this time turned against the Germans themselves. (See Reading No. 21.) Ernest Renan, the representative intellectual of France in the 1870's who until 1870/71 had deeply admired German scholarship and literature, maintained that only a close alliance between France, Germany and Britain, and not Bismarck's League of the three Eastern Emperors could guarantee European peace and liberty. (See Reading No. 22.) But in Bismarckian and Wilhelminian victorious Germany a political anti-liberal and anti-Western philosophy gained the upper hand which stressed the beneficial character of war and of a conservative state based upon a military monarchy and aristocracy. The main academic spokesman of this attitude was the historian Heinrich von Treitschke, who was immensely popular in his days. His lectures at the University of Berlin, where he occupied Ranke's chair after 1874, influenced a whole generation of high school teachers in the last third of the nineteenth century.

---

* See the much more strongly expressed fears for the future of Germany expressed by liberal German nationalists like Georg Gottfried Gervinus (1805-1871) and Georg Herwegh (1817-1875) in Kohn, The Mind of Germany (New York: Harper Torch Books, 1965), pp. 168-175.

The Prussian victories of 1866 and 1870 seemed to confirm his views and were regarded as God's judgment in history. Treitschke's views expressed the spirit which became dominant in the great war of 1914. In reality they undermined not only the unity of Europe but also her civilization and her position as the mistress of the world. (*See Reading No. 23.*)

Part II

SELECTED READINGS

Wallace: The Importance of Darwin*

Alfred Russell Wallace (1823-1913) supported Darwin's theories by his evidence from biogeography, especially in his The Geographical Distribution of Animals *(1876). In a more popular book of his, he masterfully explained the importance of Darwinism.*

The point I wish especially to urge is this. Before Darwin's work appeared, the great majority of naturalists, and almost without exception the whole literary and scientific world, held firmly to the belief that species were realities, and had not been derived from other species by any process accessible to us; the different species of crow and of violet were believed to have been always as distinct and separate as they are now, and to have originated by some totally unknown process so far removed from ordinary reproduction that it was usually spoken of as "special creation." There was, then, no question of the origin of families, orders, and classes, because the very first step of all, the "origin of species," was believed to be an insoluble problem. But now this is all changed. The whole scientific and literary world, even the whole educated public, accepts, as a matter of common knowledge, the origin by the ordinary process of natural birth. The idea of special creation or any altogether exceptional mode of production is absolutely extinct! Yet more: this is held also to apply to many higher groups as well as to the species of a genus, and not even Mr. Darwin's severest critics venture to suggest that the primeval bird, reptile, or fish must have been "specially created." And this vast, this totally unprecedented change in public opinion has been the result of the work of one man, and was brought about in the short space of twenty years! This is the answer to those who continue to maintain that the "origin of species" is not yet dis-

* Alfred Russell Wallace, *Darwinism* (London: Macmillan, 1889).

covered; that there are still doubts and difficulties; that there are divergencies of structure so great that we cannot understand how they had their beginning. We may admit all this, just as we may admit that there are enormous difficulties in the way of a complete comprehension of the origin and nature of all the parts of the solar system and of the stellar universe. But we claim for Darwin that he is the Newton of natural history, and that, just so surely as that the discovery and demonstration by Newton of the law of gravitation established order in place of chaos and laid a sure foundation for all future study of starry heavens, so surely has Darwin, by his discovery of the law of natural selection and his demonstration of the great principle of the preservation of useful variations in the struggle for life, not only thrown a flood of light on the process of development of the whole organic world, but also established a firm foundation for all future study of nature.

In order to show the view Darwin took of his work, and what it was that he alone claimed to have done, the concluding passage of the introduction to the *Origin of Species* should be carefully considered. It is as follows:

Although much remains obscure, and will long remain obscure, I can entertain no doubt, after the most deliberate and dispassionate judgment of which I am capable, that the view which most naturalists until recently entertained and which I formerly entertained—namely, that each species has been independently created —is erroneous. I am fully convinced that species are not immutable; but that those belonging to what are called the same genera are lineal descendants of some other and generally extinct species, in the same manner as the acknowledged varieties of any one species are the descendants of that species. Furthermore, I am convinced that Natural Science has been the most important, but not the exclusive, means of modification.

It should be especially noted that all which is here claimed is now almost universally admitted, while the criticisms of Darwin's works refer almost exclusively to those numerous questions which, as he himself says, "will long remain obscure . . ."

The theory of natural selection rests on two main classes of facts which apply to all organised beings without exception, and which thus take rank as fundamental principles of laws. The first is, the power of rapid multiplication in a geometrical progression; the second, that the offspring always vary slightly from the parents, though generally very loosely resembling them. From the first fact or law there follows, necessarily, a constant struggle for existence; because, while the offspring, always exceed the parents in number, generally to an enormous extent, yet the total number of living organisms in the world does not, and cannot, increase year by year. Consequently every year, on the average, as many die as are born, plants as well as animals; and the majority die premature deaths. They kill each other in a thousand different ways; they starve each other by some consuming the food that others want; they are destroyed largely by the powers of nature—by cold and heat, by rain and storm, by flood and fire. There is thus a perpetual struggle among them which shall live and which shall die; and this struggle is tremendously severe, because so few can possibly remain alive— one in five, one in ten, often only one in a hundred or even one in a thousand.

Then comes the question. Why do some live rather than others? If all the individuals of each species were exactly alike in every respect, we could only say it is a matter of chance. But they are not alike. We find that they vary in many different ways. Some are stronger, some swifter, some hardier in constitution, some more cunning. An obscure colour may render concealment more easy for some, keener sight may enable others to discover prey or escape from an enemy better than their fellows. Among plants the smallest differences may be useful or the reverse. The earliest and strongest shoots may escape the slug; their greater vigour may enable them to flower and seed earlier in a wet autumn; plants best armed with spines or hairs may escape being devoured; those whose flowers are most conspicuous may be soonest fertilised by insects. We cannot doubt that, on the whole, any beneficial variations will give the possessors of it a greater probability of living through the tremendous ordeal they have to undergo. There may be something left to chance, but on the whole the fittest will survive.

Wallace: Serfs and Emancipation in Russia*

The observations which Sir Donald Mackenzie Wallace (1841-1919) made about the conditions and life of the Russian peasants before and immediately after their emancipation (1861) are of great importance.

As to the means which the proprietors possessed of oppressing their peasants, we must distinguish between the legal and the actual. The legal were almost as complete as any one could desire. "The proprietor," it is said in the Laws (Vol. IZ., 1045, ed. an. 1857), "may impose on the serfs every kind of labor, may take from them money dues (obrok) and demand from them personal service, with this one restriction, that they should not be thereby ruined, and that the number of days fixed by law should be left to them for their own work." Besides this, he had the right to transform peasants into domestic servants, and might, instead of employing them in his own service, hire them out to others who had the rights and privileges of noblesse (1047-48). For all offenses committed against himself or against any one under his jurisdiction, he could subject the guilty ones to corporal punishment not exceeding forty lashes with the birch or fifteen blows with the stick (1052); and if he considered any of his serfs as incorrigible he could present them to the authorities to be drafted into the army or transported to Siberia as he might desire (1053-55). In cases of insubordination, where the ordinary domestic means of discipline did not suffice, he could call in the police and the military to support his authority.

Such were the legal means by which the proprietor might op-

* From D. M. Wallace, *Russia* (New York: Holt & Co., 1877), pp. 478ff., 500ff.

press his peasants, and it will be readily understood that they were very considerable and very elastic. By law he had the power to impose any dues in labor of money which he might think fit, and in all cases the serfs were ordered to be docile and obedient (1027). Corporal punishment, though restricted by law, he could in reality apply to any extent. Certainly none of the serfs, and very few of the proprietors, were aware that the law placed any restriction on this right. All the proprietors were in the habit of using corporal punishment as they thought proper, and unless a proprietor became notorious for inhuman cruelty, the authorities never thought of interfering. But in the eyes of the peasants corporal punishment was not the worst. What they feared infinitely more than the birch or the stick was the proprietor's power of giving them or their sons as recruits. The law assumed that this extreme means would be employed only against those serfs who showed themselves incorrigibly vicious or insubordinate; but the authorities accepted those presented without making any investigations, and consequently the proprietor might use his power as an effective means of extortion.

Against these means of extortion and oppression the serfs had no legal protection. The law provided them with no means of resisting any injustice to which they might be subjected, or of bringing to punishment the master who oppressed and ruined them. The Government, notwithstanding its sincere desire to protect them from inordinate burdens and cruel treatment, rarely interfered between the master and his serfs, being afraid of thereby undermining the authority of the proprietors and awakening among the peasantry a spirit of insubordination. The serfs were left, therefore, to their own resources, and had to defend themselves as best they could. The simplest way was open mutiny; but this was rarely employed, for they knew by experience that any attempt of the kind would be at once put down by the military and mercilessly punished. Much more favorite and efficient methods were passive resistance, flight, and rise-raising or murder.

We might naturally suppose that an unscrupulous proprietor, armed with the enormous legal and actual power which I have just described, could easily extort from his peasants anything he desired. In reality, however, the process of extortion, when it exceeded a certain measure, was a very difficult operation. The Russian peasant has a capacity of patient endurance, that would do honor to a martyr, and a power of continued, dogged, passive resistance such as is possessed, I believe, by no other class of men in Europe; and these qualities formed a very powerful barrier against the rapacity of unconscientious proprietors.

In speaking of the serfs I have hitherto confined my attention to the members of the Mir, or rural Commune— that is to say, the peasants in the narrower sense of the terms; but besides these there were the Dvorovye, or domestic servants, and of these I must add a word or two.

The Dvorovye were domestic slaves rather than serfs in the proper sense of the word. Let us, however, avoid wounding unnecessarily Russian sensibilities by the use of the ill-sounding word. We may call the class in question "domestics"—remembering, of course, that they were not quite domestic servants in the ordinary sense. They received no wages, were not at liberty to change masters, possessed almost no legal rights, and might be punished, hired out, or sold by their owners without any infraction of the written law.

These "domestics" were very numerous—out of all proportion to the work to be performed—and could consequently lead a very lazy life; but the peasant considered it a great misfortune to be transferred to their ranks, for he thereby lost his share of the Communal land and the little independence which he enjoyed. . . .

It might be reasonably supposed that the serfs received with boundless gratitude and delight the Manifest [of emancipation]. Here at last was the realization of their long cherished hopes. Liberty was accorded to them, and not only liberty, but a goodly portion of the soil—more than a half or all the arable land possessed by the proprietors.

In reality the Manifesto created among the peasantry a feeling of disappointment rather than delight. To understand this strange fact we must endeavor to place ourselves at the peasant's point of view.

In the first place, it must be remarked that all vague, rhetorical phrases about free labor, human dignity, national progress, and the like, which may readily produce among educated men a certain amount of temporary enthusiasm fall on the ears of the Russian peasant like drops of rain on a granite rock. If, therefore, the Government would make a law by which his share of the Communal land would be increased, or his share of the Communal burdens diminished, he would in return willingly consent to be therein designated by the most ugly name that learned ingenuity can devise.

In their minds the proprietors were merely temporary occupants, who were allowed by the Tsar to exact labor and dues from the serfs. What then was Emancipation? Certainly the abolition of all obligatory labor and money dues, and perhaps the complete ejectment of the proprietors. On this latter point there was a difference of opinion. All assumed, as a matter of course, that the Communal land would remain the property of the Commune, but it was not so clear what would be done with the rest of the estate. Some thought that it would be retained by the proprietor, but very many believed that the nobles would receive salaries from the Tsar, and that all the land would be given to the Communes. In this way the Emancipation would be in accordance with historical right and with the material advantage of the peasantry, for whose exclusive benefit, it was assumed, the reform had been undertaken. Instead of this the peasants found that they were still to pay dues, even for the Communal land which they regarded as unquestionably their own! So at least said the expounders of the law. But the thing was incredible. Either the proprietors must be concealing or misinterpreting the law, or this was merely a preparatory measure, which would be followed by the real Emancipation. Thus were awakened among the peasantry a spirit of mistrust and suspicion and a widespread belief that there would be a second Emancipation, by which all the land would be divided and all the dues abolished. . . .

The peasants naturally imagined that, as soon as the Tsar said they were free, they were no longer obliged to work for their old masters—that all obligatory labor ceased as soon as the Manifesto was read. In vain the proprietors endeavored to convince them that, in regard to labor, the old relations must continue, as the law enjoined, until a new arrangement had been made. To all explanations and exhortations the peasants turned a deaf ear, and to the efforts of the rural police they too often opposed a dogged, passive resistance. In many cases the simple appearance of the authorities sufficed to restore order, for the presence of one of the Tsar's servants convinced many that the order to work for the present as formerly was not a mere invention of the proprietors. But not unfrequently the birch had to be applied. Indeed, I am inclined to believe, from the numerous descriptions of this time which I have received from eye-witnesses, that rarely, if ever, had the serfs seen and experienced so much flogging as during these first three months after their liberation. . . .

At first the work of amicable settlement proceeded slowly. The proprietors generally showed a spirit of concession, and some of them generously proposed conditions much more favorable to the peasants than the law demanded; but the peasants were filled with vague suspicions, and feared to commit themselves by "putting pen to paper." Even the highly-respected proprietors, who imagined that they possessed the unbounded confidence of the peasantry, were suspected like the others, and their generous offers were regarded as ill-baited traps. Often I have heard old men, sometimes with tears in their eyes, describe the distrust and ingratitude of the peasantry at this time. Many peasants believed that the proprietors were hiding the real Emancipation Law, and imaginative or ill-intentioned persons fostered this belief by professing to know what the real law contained. The most absurd rumors were afloat, and whole villages sometimes acted upon them. In the province of Moscow, for instance, one Commune sent a deputation to the proprietor to inform him that, as he had always been a good master, the Mir would allow him to retain his house and garden during his lifetime. In another locality it was rumored that the Tsar sat daily on a golden throne in the Crimea, receiving all peasants who came to him, and giving them as much land as they desired, and in order to take advantage of the Imperial liberality a large body of peasants set out for the place indicated, and advanced quickly till they were stopped by the military!

The work of concluding contracts for the redemption of the dues, or, in other words, for the purchase of the land ceded in perpetual usufruct, proceeded slowly, and is, in fact, still going on. The arrangement was as follows: The dues were capitalized at six per cent, and the Government paid at once to the proprietors four-fifths of the remaining fifth, either at once or in installments, and to the Government six per cent, for forty-nine years on the sum advanced. The proprietors willingly adopted this arrangement, for it provided them with a sum of ready money, and freed them from the difficult task of collecting the dues. But the peasants did not show much desire to undertake the operation. Some of them expected a second emancipation, and those who did not take this possibility into their calculations were little disposed to make present sacrifices for distant prospective advantages which would not be realized for half a century. In most cases the proprietor was obliged to remit, in whole or in part, the fifth which was to be paid by the peasants. Many Communes refused to undertake the operation on any conditions, and in consequence of this not few proprietors demanded the so-called obligatory redemption, according to which they accepted the four-fifths from the Government as full payment, and the operation was thus effected without the peasants being consulted. The total number of male serfs emancipated was about nine millions and three-quarters, and of these, only about seven millions and a quarter had already, at the beginning of 1875, made redemption contracts. Of the contracts signed at that time, about sixty-three per cent were "obligatory." . . .

Veuillot: Ultramontane Catholicism*

In 1866 Louis Veuillot published a pamphlet in which he advanced his opposition to liberal Catholicism. Veuillot maintained that the liberal illusion is not only empty, but that its counsels to the Catholic world of a reconciliation with modern civilization are weak and dishonest recommendations which disclose the ignoble mainspring of liberal Catholicism.

The children of the Christ, the children of the King, are kings. They form an absolutely superior society, whose duty it is to take possession of the earth and reign over it for the purpose of baptizing all men and of raising them to that selfsame supernatural life, that selfsame royalty and that selfsame glory for which Christ has destined them. They ought to strive for that goal, because the only way of realizing the ideal of universal liberty, universal equality, universal fraternity is to establish the universal reign of Christ. For the liberty that is man's due is liberty to attain his supernatural end, which is union with Christ; and the only society ever known to recognize all men as equals and as brothers is the society of the disciples of Christ.

In the normal order, Christian society is maintained and extended by means of two powers that ought to be distinct—not separated, united—not confused, one above the other—not equal. The one is the head, the other the arm; the one is the supreme and sovereign word of the Pontiff, the other the social power. . . .

These two powers, united, distinct and one above the other, whereby Christian society is ruled, have been called the two swords. For the word would be of no avail, if it could not be at certain moments a sword. The meekness of Christ has willed

* Louis Veuillot, *The Liberal Illusion,* tr. by George Barry O'Toole, (Washington: National Catholic Conference, 1939). Reprinted by permission of the publisher, pp. 37-38, 38-39, 47-48, 62-64, 76-77.

that there should be two swords, so that the advent of repression might be delayed and the need of it forestalled.

The first sword, the one that cleaves nothing but darkness, remains in the patient and infallibly enlightened power of the Pontiff. The other, the material sword, is in the hand of the representative of society, and in order that it may make no mistake, it is in duty bound to obey the commandment of the Pontiff. It is the Pontiff who bids it come forth from the scabbard and who bids it return thereto. Its duty is to repress aggressive error, once it has been defined and condemned, to shackle it, to strike it down; to give protection to the truth, whether the latter is under the necessity of defending itself, or has need in its turn, to go on the offensive. . . .

The Christians despoiled pagan society of its weapons and its temples to transform them, not to destroy them. From the temple, they expelled the idol; upon might they imposed right. The foolish idea of abolishing force never even came to them. Force allowed itself to be transposed, allowed itself to be disciplined; allowed itself to be sanctified. Who is so rash as to think he can abolish might? and why, after all, should anyone wish to abolish it at all? Might is a very good thing; it is a gift of God, nay a very attribute of God, "I am the most mighty God of thy father."

As right is of itself a force, so force can be of itself a right. Mankind and the Church recognize a right of war. From the iron of which it despoiled barbarous force, Christianity made coats of mail for the weak and noble swords with which it armed the right. Force in the hands of the Church is the force of right, and we have no desire that right should remain without force. Force in its proper place and doing its duty, that is the orderly way.

Because in the present world force is not everywhere in its proper place, that is to say at the disposition of the Church; because often, far from serving right, it is abused against the right, shall we therefore say yes to the illuminati, some of whom decree the outright abolition of force, while the rest ordain that the supreme right shall never have force at its disposal, for fear it might hamper the liberty that wants to destroy the truth?

We ought, on the contrary, to be ready to shed our blood in

order to restore force to its lawful function, in order to attach it exclusively to the service of right.

Force ought to protect, to affirm, to vindicate the grandest, the noblest, the most necessary right of man, which is to acknowledge and to serve God; it should enable the Church to extend to every man on earth the benefit of this right. Let us never relinquish this right which liberal Catholicism surrenders, so that it can drift down the current, along with the crowd. . . .

The revolutionary sphinx, under the name of the modern mind, propounds a series of riddles with which the liberal Catholics occupy themselves a great deal more than befits the dignity of children of Christ. Not one of them, however, answers the riddle in a way calculated to satisfy either the sphinx or themselves, or anybody else, and it is a matter of record, that the monster devours soonest just those who flatter themselves on having guessed its meaning best.

Scant is the self-respect and scant the faith that remains in these last! They come, not without arrogance, to ask, in the name of the sphinx and in their own name, how "intolerant" Catholics can get around the "conquests" of the dissenting mind with its rights of man, its liberty of religions, its constitutions grounded on these principles, etc., etc. Nothing could be easier to answer.

To begin with, the dissenting mind invariably starts off with an unwarranted assumption of its own superiority, which we flatly refuse to recognize. Error is never the equal, much less the superior of truth, neither can it hope to overawe truth, or ever to prevail legitimately against it, and, by consequence, the disciples of error, infidels, unbelievers, atheists, renegades, and the like, are never the superiors nor even the legitimate equals of the disciples of Jesus Christ, the one true God. From the standpoint of unalterable right, the perfect society that constitutes the Church of Christ is by no means on a level with the gang that collects around error. We know right well to whom it has been said: Going therefrom, teach—a word, we may remark in passing, like the great Increase and multiply, which was spoken at the beginning of things; and these two words are living words despite the ruses and triumphs of death—error has nothing to increase and multiply. Truth is at liberty to tolerate error, but error is obliged to grant to truth the right of liberty. . . .

In a word, Catholic society will be Catholic, and the dissenters whom it will tolerate will know its charity, but they will not be allowed to disrupt its unity.

This is the answer that Catholics can, on their part, make to the sphinx; and these are the words that will kill it outright. The sphinx is not unvulnerable; against it we have just what is required in the way of weapons. The Archangel did not overcome the Rebel with material weapons, but with this word: Who is like unto God! And Satan fell, struck as by a bolt of lightning. . . .

It is only too evident that, considering the present state of the world, liberal Catholicism has no value whatever either as a doctrine or as a means of defending religion; that it is powerless to insure for the Church a peace which would bring her the least advancement or glory. It is nothing but an illusion, nothing but a piece of stubbornness—a pose. One can predict its fate. Abandoned in the near future by generous minds, to whom it may provide a certain outlet for sentiment, it will go on to merge itself with the general body of heresy. The adherents whom it drags after it may then be turned into fanatical persecutors, in keeping with the usual inconsistency of weak intellects obsessed with the false spirit of conciliation! Certain minds seem to be as susceptible to error as certain constitutions to disease. Everything that is unwholesome finds lodgment in them; they are carried away by the very first wind and ensnared by the very first sophism; they are the property, the booty, the chattels of the powers of darkness, and one may define them as antiquity defined slaves, *non tam viles quam nulli*—"not so much vile beings as nobodies."

Let us undertake not so much to convince them as to set them an example that may save them.

In harmony with faith, reason exhorts us to unite and make ourselves strong in obedience. To whom shall we go? Liberals or not liberals, beset with the terrible perplexities of these troublous times, we know only one thing for a certainty: it is that no man knows anything, except the man with whom God is for aye, the man who possesses the thought of God.

It behooves us to lock arms around the Sovereign Pontiff, to follow unswervingly his inspired directions, to affirm with him the truths that alone can save our souls and the world. It behooves us to abstain from any attempt to twist his words to our own sense: "When the Sovereign Pontiff has proclaimed a pastoral decision, no one has the right to add or to suppress the smallest vowel, *no addere, no minuere*. Whatever he affirms, that is true forever." Any other course can but result in dividing us further and in fatally disrupting our unity. That is the misfortune of misfortunes. The doctrines known as liberal have riven us apart. Before their inroad, favored only too much, alas! by a spell of political bad humor, few as we were, we amounted, nevertheless, to something: we formed an unbroken phalanx. We rallied in such a phalanx whenever we chose to do so; it was no more than a pebble if you will: that pebble had at least its compactness and its weight. Liberalism has shattered it and reduced it to so much dust. I doubt if it still holds its place: dispersal is not expansion. At all events, a hundred thousand pecks of dust would not furnish ammunition for a single sling. Let us aim now at but one goal, let us work with but one mind to attain it: let us throw ourselves wholeheartedly into obedience; it will give us the cohesion of rock, and upon this rock, *hanc petram*, Truth shall plant her victorious foot.

The Unification of Italy*

After the constitution of the Kingdom of Italy in February 1861, the Roman Question embittered the relations between the Papacy and Italian nationalism. On the one hand the Italian Prime Minister Baron Bettino Ricasoli (1809-80), who had engineered the annexation of his native Tuscany to Sardinia, claimed Rome openly for Italy, (A); on the other hand, Pope Pius IX clung to the "sacred property of the church" (B).

(A) Italy's Claims

But the king's government sees a territory to defend and a territory to recover. It sees Rome; it sees Venice! To the Eternal City and to the Queen of the Adriatic it directs the thoughts, the hopes, and the energies of the nation. The government feels the heavy task that lies before it; with God's help it will fulfill it. Opportunity matured by time will open our way to Venice. In the meantime we think of Rome.

Yes, we will go to Rome. Shall Rome, politically severed from the rest of Italy, continue to be the center of intrigue and conspiracy, a permanent threat to public order? To go to Rome is for the Italians not merely a right; it is an inexorable necessity. The king's government will be frank and clear upon this matter, even more than upon any other subject. We do not wish to go to Rome through insurrectional movements,—unreasonable, rash, mad attempts,—which may endanger our former acquisitions and ruin the national enterprise. We will go to Rome hand in hand with France!

(B) The Pope's Protest

A Catholic king, forgetful of every religious principle, despising every right, trampling upon every law, after having, little by little, despoiled the august head of the Catholic Church of

* *Annual Register* (1861), Section "History," pp. 187, 190.

the greatest and most flourishing portion of his legitimate possessions, has now taken to himself the title of King of Italy, with which title he has sought to seal the sacrilegious usurpations already consummated,—usurpations which his government has already manifested its intention of completing to the detriment of the patrimony of the apostolic see. Although the Holy Father has solemnly protested against the successive attacks made upon his sovereignty, he is nevertheless under the obligation of issuing a fresh protest against the assumption of a title tending to legitimize the iniquity of so many deeds.

It would here be superfluous to recall the sacred character of the possessions of the Church's patrimony and the right of the supreme pontiff to it,—an incontestable right, recognized at all times and by all governments. Therefore the Holy Father will never be able to recognize the title of King of Italy, arrogated to himself by the king of Sardinia, since it is opposed to justice and to the sacred property of the Church. On the contrary, he makes the most ample and formal protest against such an usurpation.

Bismarck's Territorial Claims*

The dangers of Bismarck's policy for the peace of Europe were clearly foreseen after the Gastein Conference in the summer of 1865 between Austria and Prussia about the future of Schleswig-Holstein. The (London) Times wrote in an editorial of September 13, 1865 as follows:

It is highly improbable that any of his successors will ever recur to his Napoleonic idea; but we wish we could add with truth that such fraudulent and arbitrary proceedings as those whereby the First Napoleon compassed his aims are no longer possible in modern Europe. The morality of the Gastein-Convention resembles too nearly the morality of the Bayonne interview for us to indulge in any such self-congratulations. It is now evident that under pretexts as hollow as those which masked Napoleon's vast projects of dismemberment and spoliation, M. Bismarck has been plotting the partition of the Danish Monarchy for the benefit of Prussia. The indissoluble union of Schleswig and Holstein was the very basis of the intervention. The one province has been assigned to Austria and the other to Prussia. The claims of the House of Oldenburg, the House of Augustenburg, or any other House that would serve the turn, were put forward with pompous insincerity against those of the reigning House of Denmark; it now turns out that all were to be ignored as soon as Prussia was fairly in possession. The right of the Schleswig-Holsteiners to choose their own Government was strongly asserted, and was, indeed, by far the best argument on the German side; it is now utterly and deliberately cast aside. It is strange and melancholy that a policy so perilous to the peace of Europe should be revived, not by the "ancient enemy," but by the "natural allies" of Great Britain. It warns us that even in the present day we must rely on the fear of consequences alone to restrain the imperious instinct of territorial aggrandisement.

* *The Times* (London), September 13, 1865.

Bismarck and the Ems Dispatch*

*In the evening of July 13, 1870, Bismarck received the dispatch sent on behalf of King William I by Heinrich Abeken (1809-1782), a member of the Prussian foreign office staff, from Bad Ems. The dispatch reported on the King's encounter with the French ambassador. About the impression made on Bismarck and his two dinner guests that evening Bismarck himself reported in his Memoirs.**

I invited Generals Moltke and Roon to have dinner with me on July 13th, and spoke to them concerning my views and intentions. During the dinner conversation it was reported to me that a code telegram had been received from Ems, and it was then in process of decoding. I then read it to my guests, who were so crushed that they refused to eat or drink.

All considerations, conscious or unconscious, strengthened my opinion that war could be avoided only at the cost of the honor of Prussia and of the national confidence in her.

Under this conviction I made use of the royal authority communicated to me through Abeken to publish the contents of the telegram. In the presence of my guests I reduced the telegram by deleting words, but without adding or altering a single word. . . .

The difference in the effect of the shortened text of the Ems telegram as compared with that of the original was not the result of stronger words but of the form, which made the announcement appear decisive.

* Otto von Bismarck, *Gedanken und Erinnerungen* (Stuttgart, 1898), Vol. II, pp. 406-408. See the discussion of the whole problem in the abbreviated and critically annotated edition by A. M. Gibson (Cambridge University Press, 1940) Chapter XIV and Annex II. See also Lawrence D. Steefel, *Bismarck, the Hohenzollern Candidacy, and the Origins of the Franco-German War of 1870* (Cambridge: Harvard University Press, 1962).

After I had read the condensed version to my two guests, Moltke said:

"Now it has a quite different ring. In its original form it sounded like a parley. Now it is like a flourish of trumpets in answer to a challenge!"

I went on to explain:

"If, in execution of His Majesty's order, I immediately communicate this text, which contains no changes in or additions to the telegram, not only to the newpapers but also by wire to all our embassies, it will be known in Paris before midnight. Not only on account of the contents but also because of the manner of its distribution, it will have the effect of a red flag on the Gallic bull.

"We must fight if we do not want to act the part of the defeated without a battle. However, success depends essentially upon the impression which the beginning of the war makes upon us and others. It is not important that we should be the ones attacked. Gallic insolence and sensitivity will bring this about if we announce before all Europe, as far as we can without the speaking tube of the Reichstag, that we are courageously meeting the public threats of France."

This explanation drew from both generals a metamorphosis into a more joyous mood, whose liveliness surprised me. They had suddenly recovered their desire to eat and drink and began to speak in a more cheerful tone.

Roon said: "Our God of old still lives, and will not let us die in disgrace."

Moltke relinquished his passive equanimity so much that, glancing up joyously to the ceiling and abandoning his usual punctiliousness of speech, he pounded his chest with his hand and exclaimed:

"If I may but live to lead our armies in such a war, then right afterwards let the devil come and haul away the old carcass." He was then more frail that later and had his doubts as to whether he could live through the fatigue of a field campaign.

Gladstone for the Extension of the Vote*

In the House of Commons Gladstone spoke in support of his bill to enlarge the suffrage in 1866.

Let us consider the enormous and silent changes which have been going forward among the laboring population. May I use the words to honorable and right honorable gentlemen once used by way of exhortation by Sir Robert Peel, "Elevate your vision"? Let us try and raise our views above the fears, suspicions, jealousies, attacks, and recriminations of this place. Let us look onward to the time of our children and our children's children. Is there or is there not a steady movement of the laboring classes, and is or is not that movement onwards and upwards? I do not say you can see it; for, like all great processes, it is unobservable in detail but solid and unassailable in character. It is like those movements of the earth's crust, which science tells us are even now going on in certain portions of the globe, which sailors sail over and the traveler by land treads upon without being conscious of them; but science tells you that the changes are taking place, and that things are not as they were. Has my right honorable friend ever considered the astonishing phenomena connected with some portion of the conduct of the laboring classes, and especially in the Lancashire distress? Has he considered what an amount of self-denial was exhibited by these men in respect to the American [civil] war? Could any man have believed that a conduct so still, so calm, so firm, so energetic, could have planted itself in the minds of a population without becoming a known patent fact through the whole country? And yet when the day of trial came, we saw that noble sympathy on their part with the people of the North; that determination that, be their sufferings what they might, no word should proceed from them that would damage a cause

* *Annual Register,* 1866, pp. 130-135.

so just. On one side, there was a magnificent moral spectacle; on the other side, there was a great lesson to us all, to teach us that, in their minds, by a process of quiet instillation, opinions and sentiments were gradually forming themselves, of which we for a long time remain unaware, but that, when at last they make their appearance, are found mature, solid, and irresistible. . . .

You cannot fight against the future. Time is on our side. The great social forces which move on in their might and majesty, and which the tumult of our debates does not for a moment impede or disturb,—those great social forces are against you; they are marshaled on our side; and the banner which we now carry, though, perhaps, at some moment it may droop over our sinking heads, yet it soon again will float in the eye of heaven, and it will be borne by the firm hands of the united people of the three kingdoms, perhaps not to an easy but to a certain and to a not distant victory.

John Bright: British Labor and the American Civil War*

In 1861-1865 the British textile industry in Lancashire, historically the most important branch of British industry, suffered bitterly from the non-availability of its raw material imported from the southern United States. Large-scale unemployment was the result. But whereas the upper classes in Britain sympathized with the Confederacy, labor in Lancashire steadfastly took the side of the Union. John Bright explained the pro-Union position on December 4, 1861 at a dinner in Rochdale, a cotton-spinning borough in Lancashire, where Bright was born.

In these times in which we live, by the influence of the telegraph and the steamboat and the railroad, and the multiplication of newspapers, we seem continually to stand as on the top of an exceedingly high mountain, from which we behold all the kingdoms of the earth and the glory of them—unhappily, also, not only their glory, but their follies and their crimes and their calamities.

Seven years ago our eyes were turned with anxious expectation to a remote corner of Europe,† where five nations were contending in bloody strife for an object which possibly hardly one of them comprehended, and, if they did comprehend it, which all sensible men amongst them must have known to be absolutely impracticable. Four years ago we were looking still further to the east,‡ where there was a gigantic revolt in a great dependency of the British crown, arising mainly from gross neglect, and from the incapacity of England, up to that moment, to govern the country which it had known how to conquer. Two years ago we

* John Bright at a dinner on December 4, 1861, in Rochdale, a cotton-spinning borough in Lancashire.
† Reference to the Crimean War (1854).
‡ Reference to the Indian Mutiny (1857).

looked south, to the plains of Lombardy, and saw a great strife there, in which every man of England took a strong interest; and we have welcomed, as the results of that strife, the addition of a great kingdom to the list of European states. Now our eyes are turned in a contrary direction and we look to the west. There we see a struggle in progress of the very highest interest to England and to humanity at large. We see there a nation which I shall call the transatlantic English nation—the inheritor and partaker of all the historic glories of this country. We see it torn with intestine broils and suffering from calamities from which for more than a century past, in fact, for more than two centuries past, this country has been exempt. That struggle is of especial interest to us. We remember the description which one of our great poets gives of Rome, "Lone mother of dead empires."

But England is the living mother of great nations on the American and on the Australian continents, which promise to endow the world with all her knowledge and all her civilization, and with even something more than the freedom she herself enjoys. . . .

Now I am obliged to say, and I say it with the utmost pain, that if we have not done things which are plainly hostile to the North, and if we have not expressed affection for slavery and, outwardly and openly, hatred for the Union,—I say that there has not been that friendly and cordial neutrality which, if I had been a citizen of the United States, I should have expected; and I say further, that, if there has existed considerable irritation at that, it must be taken as a measure of the high appreciation which the people of those states place upon the opinion of the people of England. If I had been addressing this audience ten days ago, so far as I know, I should have said just what I have said now; and although, by an untoward event, circumstances are somewhat, even considerably, altered, yet I have thought it desirable to make this statement, with a view, so far as I am able to do it, to improve the opinion of England and to assuage feelings of irritation in America, if there be any, so that no further difficulties may arise in the progress of this unhappy strife. . . .

Remembering the past, remembering at this moment the perils

of a friendly people, and seeing the difficulties by which they are surrounded, let us, I entreat of you, see if there be any real moderation in the people of England, and if magnanimity, so often to be found amongst individuals, is absolutely wanting in a great nation. . . .

Now, whether the Union will be restored or not, or the South achieve an unhonoured independence or not, I know not and I predict not. But this I think I know, that in a few years, a very few years, the twenty millions of freemen in the North will be thirty millions, or even fifty millions—a population equal to or exceeding that of this kingdom. When that time comes I pray that it may not be said amongst them that in the darkest hour of their country's trials England, the land of their fathers, looked on with icy coldness and saw unmoved the perils and calamities of their children. As for me, I have but this to say: I am but one in this audience, and but one in the citizenship of this country; but if all other tongues are silent, mine shall speak for that policy which gives hope to the bondmen of the South, and which tends to generous thoughts and generous deeds between the two great nations who speak the English language, and from their origin are alike entitled to the English name.

Gladstone on Classical Languages*

*In the 1860's the rival claims of the traditional classical train-
ing and the acquisition of modern knowledge were widely discussed in Europe. Here two letters by Gladstone are reproduced
on the place of classical learning in the human culture of the
mid-Victorian age.*

Mr. Gladstone to Lord Lyttelton

Penmaenmawr, August 29, 1861.—Thanks for the brief notice
which you recently took of the Public Schools Commission. I
was heartily glad to hear that you had formed a drastic set of
questions. I take the deepest interest in the object of the commission, and I have full confidence in its members and organs;
and at all times I shall be very glad to hear what you are doing.
Meantime I cannot help giving you, to be taken for what it is
worth, the sum of my own thoughts upon the subject. . . . The
low utilitarian argument in matter of education, for giving it
what is termed a practical direction, is so plausible that I think
we may on the whole be thankful that the instincts of the country have resisted what in argument it has been ill able to con-
fute. We still hold by the classical training as the basis of a liberal education; parents dispose of their children in early youth
accordingly; but if they were asked why they did so, it is probable they would give lamentably weak or unworthy reasons for
it, such for example as that the public schools and universities
open the way to desirable acquaintance and what is termed 'good
society.' Your commission will not I presume be able to pass by
this question, but will have to look it in the face; and to proceed
either upon a distinct affirmative, or a substantial negative, of
the proposition that the classical training is the proper basis of

* John Morley, *The Life of William Ewart Gladstone,* Vol. II (New
York: The Macmillan Company, 1903), pp. 646-649.

a liberal education. I hope you will hold by affirmation and reject negation.

But the reason why I trouble you upon the subject is this, that I think the friends of this principle have usually rather blinked the discussion, and have been content with making terms of compromise by way of buying off the adversary, which might be in themselves reasonable unless they were taken as mere instalments of a transaction intended in the long run to swallow up the principle itself. What I feel is that the relation of pure science, natural science, modern languages, modern history, and the rest of the old classical training ought to be founded on a principle and ought not to be treated simply as importunate creditors, that take a shilling in the £ to-day, because they hope to get another shilling to-morrow, and in the meantime have a recognition of their title. This recognition of title is just what I would refuse. I deny their right to a parallel or equal position; their true position is auxiliary, and as auxiliary it ought to be limited and restrained without scruple, as a regard to the paramount matter of education may dictate.

But why after all is the classical training paramount? Is it because we find it established? Because it improves memory or taste, or gives precision, or develops the faculty of speech? All these are but partial and fragmentary statements, so many narrow glimpses of a great and comprehensive truth. That truth I take to be that the modern European civilisation from the middle age downwards is the compound of two great factors, the Christian religion for the spirit of man, and the Greek, and in a secondary degree the Roman discipline for his mind and intellect. St. Paul is the apostle of the Gentiles, and is in his own person a symbol of this great wedding—the place, for example, of Aristotle and Plato in Christian education is not arbitrary nor in principle mutable. The materials of what we call classical training were prepared, and we have a right to say were advisedly prepared, in order that it might become not a mere adjunct but (in mathematical phrase) the complement of Christianity in its application to the culture of a human being formed both for this world and for the world to come.

If this principle be true it is broad and high and clear enough, and supplies a key to all questions connected with the relation between the classical training of our youth and all other branches of their secular education. It must of course be kept within its proper place, and duly limited as to things and persons. It can only apply in full to that small proportion of the youth of any country, who are to become in the fullest sense educated men. It involves no extravagant or inconvenient assumptions respecting those who are to be educated for trades and professions in which the necessities of specific training must limit general culture. It leaves open every question turning upon individual aptitudes and inaptitudes and by no means requires that boys without a capacity for imbibing any of the spirit of classical culture are still to be mechanically plied with the instruments of it after their unfitness has become manifest. But it lays down the rule of education for those who have no internal and no external disqualification; and that rule, becoming a fixed and central point in the system, becomes also the point around which all others may be grouped.

Mr. Gladstone to Sir S. Northcote

Nov. 12, 1961.—The letter I wrote to Lyttelton about the classical education suggested topics, which as you justly perceive are altogether esoteric. They have never to my knowledge been carefully worked out, and I think they well deserve it; but clearly your report is not the place. I will not say you are not prudent in suggesting that you should not even give an opinion upon the great question: What is the true place of the old classical learning in the human culture of the nineteenth century? I am far from venturing to say the contrary. But one thing I do think, namely, that it is desirable that, as far as may be, the members of the commission should have some answer to that question in their minds, and should write their report with reference to it. For centuries, through the lifetime of our great schools this classical culture has been made the *lapis angularis* of all secular culture of the highest class. Was this right or was it wrong, aye or no? I think it much to be desired that the commission should, if they will, proceed upon the affirmative or negative of that proposition, and should also make their choice for the former. This would be a long note to their report; but it need not be distinctly and separately heard in it. Such is my notion. As to particulars I have little to say that is worth hearing; but I think these three things. First, that we give much too little scope for deviation from what I think the normal standard to other and useful branches, when it has become evident that the normal standard is inapplicable; just as was the case in Oxford before the reform of the examinations, or let me rather say the new statutes. Secondly, I am extremely jealous of any invasion of modern languages which is to displace classical culture, or any portion of it in minds capable of following that walk. (I take it that among the usual modern tongues Italian has by far the greatest capacity for strict study and scholarship; whereas it is the one least in favour and the whole method of dealing with them is quite alien to strict study.) Lastly, I confess I grieve over the ignorance of natural history which I feel in myself and believe to exist in others. At some time, in some way, much more of all this ought to be brought in, but clearly it would serve in a great degree as recreation, and need not thrust aside whatever hard work boys are capable of doing.

Gladstone: His First Budget*

As the Chancellor of the Exchequer in 1853, Gladstone presented his first budget to the House of Commons on April 18, 1853. The speech, which lasted for five hours, kept the House spellbound. He defined the principles guiding him as follows:

If the Committee have followed me, they will understand that we found ourselves on the principle that the income-tax ought to be marked as a temporary measure; that the public feeling that relief should be given to intelligence and skill as compared with property ought to be pointed out; that the income-tax in its operation ought to be mitigated by every rational means, compatible with its integrity; and, above all, that it should be associated in the last term of its existence, as it was in the first, with those remissions of indirect taxation which have so greatly redounded to the profit of this country, and have set so admirable an example—an example that has already in some quarters proved contagious—to the other nations of the earth. These are the principles on which we stand, and these the figures. I have shown you that if you grant us the taxes which we ask, to the moderate amount of 2,500,000 in the whole, much less than that sum for the present year, you, or the parliament which may be in existence in 1860, will be in the condition, if it shall so think fit, to part with the income-tax.

These are the proposals of the Government. They may be approved or they may be condemned, but I have at least this full and undoubting confidence, that it will on all hands be admitted that we have not sought to evade the difficulties of our positions; that we have not attempted to counteract them by narrow or flimsy expedients; that we have prepared plans which, if you will adopt them, will go some way to close up many vexed financial questions—questions such as, if not now settled, may

* Speech of April 18, 1853.

be attended with public inconvenience, and even with public danger, in future years and under less favourable circumstances; that we have endeavoured, in the plans we have now submitted to you, to make the path of our successors in future years not more arduous but more easy; and I may be permitted to add that, while we have sought to do justice, by the changes we propose in taxation, to intelligence and skill as compared with property—while we have sought to do justice to the great labouring community of England by furthering their relief from indirect taxation, we have not been guided by any desire to put one class against another. We have felt we should best maintain our own honour, that we should best meet the views of parliament, and best promote the interests of the country, by declining to draw any invidious distinction between class and class, by adopting it to ourselves as a sacred aim to diffuse and distribute—burden if we must, benefit if we may—with equal and impartial hand; and we have the consolation of believing that by proposals such as these we contribute, as far as in us lies, not only to develop the material resources of the country, but to knit the hearts of the various classes of this great nation yet more closely than heretofore to that Throne and to those institutions under which it is their happiness to live.

The Conservative Party Program*

Disraeli delivered a speech in Manchester on April 3, 1872, in the Free Trade Hall, where he spoke to an enthusiastic audience with unflagging spirit for three hours and a quarter. This speech and its reception assured Disraeli's leadership of the party and the party's victory at the elections of 1874.

The Conservative party are accused of having no programme of policy. If by a programme is meant a plan to despoil churches and plunder landlords, I admit we have no programme. If by a programme is meant a policy which assails or menaces every institution and every interest, every class and every calling in the country, I admit we have no programme. But if to have a policy with distinct ends, and these such as most deeply interest the great body of the nation, be a becoming programme for a political party, then, I contend, we have an adequate programme, and one which, here or elsewhere, I shall always be prepared to assert and to vindicate.

Gentlemen, the programme of the Conservative party is to maintain the Constitution of the country. I have not come down to Manchester to deliver an essay on the English Constitution; but when the banner of Republicanism is unfurled—when the fundamental principles of our institutions are controverted—I think, perhaps, it may not be inconvenient that I should make some few practical remarks upon the character of our Constitution—upon that monarchy, limited by the co-ordinate authority of Estates of the realm, which, under the title of Queen, Lords and Commons, has contributed so greatly to the prosperity of this country, and with the maintenance of which I believe that prosperity is bound up.

* T. E. Kebbel, ed., *Selected Speeches of the Late Right Honourable the Earl of Beaconsfield* (2 vols., London, 1882), Vol. II, pp. 491-492, 501-502, 510-512.

Gentlemen, since the settlement of that Constitution, now nearly two centuries ago, England has never experienced a revolution, though there is no country in which there has been so continuous and such considerable change. How is this? Because the wisdom of your forefathers placed the prize of supreme power without the sphere of human passions. Whatever the struggle of parties, whatever the strife of factions, whatever the excitement and exaltation of the public mind, there has always been something in this country round which all classes and parties could rally, representing the majesty of the law, the administration of justice, and involving, at the same time, the security for every man's rights and the fountain of honour. Now, gentlemen, it is well clearly to comprehend what is meant by a country not having a revolution for two centuries. It means, for that space, the unbroken exercise and enjoyment of the ingenuity of man. It means, for that space, the continuous application of the discoveries of science to his comfort and convenience. It means the accumulation of capital, the elevation of labour, the establishment of those admirable factories which cover your district; the unwearied improvement of the cultivation of the land, which has extracted from a somewhat churlish soil harvests more exuberant than those furnished by lands nearer to the sun. It means the continuous order which is the only parent of personal liberty and political right. And you owe all these, gentlemen, to the Throne. . . .

Lord Grey, in his Reform measure of 1832, which was no doubt a statesmanlike measure, committed a great and for a time it appeared an irretrievable error. By that measure he fortified the legitimate influence of the aristocracy; but he not only made no provision for the representation of the working classes in the Constitution, but he absolutely abolished those ancient franchises which the working classes had peculiarly enjoyed and exercised from time immemorial. Gentlemen, that was the origin of Chartism, and of that electoral uneasiness which existed in this country more or less for thirty years. The Liberal party, I feel it my duty to say, had not acted fairly by this question. In their adversity they held out hopes to the working classes, but when they had a strong Government they laughed their vows to scorn. In 1848 there was a French Revolution and a Republic was established. No one can have forgotten what the effect was in this country. I remember the day when not a woman could leave her house in London, and when cannon were planted on Westminster Bridge. When Lord Derby became Prime Minister (1852) affairs had arrived at such a point that it was of the first moment that the question should be sincerely dealt with. He had to encounter great difficulties, but he accomplished his purpose with the support of a united party. And, gentlemen, what has been the result? A year ago there was another revolution in France, and a Republic was again established of the most menacing character. What happened in this country? You could not get half a dozen men to assemble in a street and grumble. Why? Because the people had got what they wanted. They were content and they were grateful. . . .

Gentlemen, I think public attention . . . ought to be concentrated upon sanitary legislation. That is a wide subject, and, if properly treated, comprises almost every consideration which has just claim upon legislative interference. Pure air, pure water, the inspection of unhealthy habitations, the adulteration of food, these and many kindred matters may be legitimately dealt with by the Legislature; and I am bound to say the Legislature is not idle upon them; for we have at this time two important measures before Parliament on the subject. One—by a late colleague of mine, Sir Charles Adderley—is a large and comprehensive measure, founded upon a sure basis, for it consolidates all existing public Acts and improves them. A prejudice has been raised against that proposal, by stating that it interferes with the private Acts of the great towns. I take this opportunity of contradicting that. The Bill of Sir Charles Adderley does not touch the Acts of the great towns. It only allows them if they think fit to avail themselves of its new provisions.

The other measure, by the government, is of a partial character. What it comprises is good, so far as it goes, but it shrinks from that bold consolidation of existing Acts which I think one of the great merits of Sir Charles Adderley's Bill, which permits us to become acquainted with how much may be done in favour of sanitary improvement by existing provisions. Gentlemen, I cannot impress upon you too strongly my conviction of the importance of the Legislature and society uniting together in favour of these important results. A great scholar and a great wit, 300 years ago, said that, in his opinion, there was a great mistake in the Vulgate, which as you know is the Latin translation of the Holy Scriptures, and that instead of saying "Vanity of vanities, all is vanity"—*Vanitas vanitatum, omnia vanitas*—the wise and witty King really said *Sanitas sanitatum, omnia sanitas*. Gentlemen, it is impossible to overrate the importance of the subject. After all, the first consideration of a minister should be the health of the people. A land may be covered with historic trophies, with museums of science and galleries of art, with universities and with libraries; the people may be civilised and ingenious; the country may be even famous in the annals and action of the world, but, gentlemen, if the population every ten years decreases, and the stature of the race every ten years diminishes, the history of that country will soon be the history of the past. . . .

Lady Beaconsfield*

These are some of the letters exchanged between Disraeli and his wife, and letters which he received after her death. They are reproduced here not only for the insight which they afford into the life and character of Disraeli but also into the style of the Victorian era. The last letter speaks also of the Queen's affection for Disraeli.

To Lady Beaconsfield

July 25, 1872.—I have nothing to tell you, except that I love you, which, I fear, you will think rather dull. . . .

Natty [Lord Rothschild] was very affectionate about you, and wanted me to come home and dine with him; quite alone; but I told him that you were the only person now, whom I could dine with; and only relinquished you to-night for my country.

My country, I fear, will be very late; but I hope to find you in a sweet sleep.

From Lady Beaconsfield

July 26

My own Dearest,—I miss you sadly. I feel so grateful for your constant tender love and kindness. I certainly feel better this evening. . . . Your own devoted Beaconsfield.

From William Ewart Gladstone

10, Downing Street, Whitehall, January 19, 1873.— . . . You and I were, as I believe, married in the same year. It has been permitted to both of us to enjoy a priceless boon through a third of a century. Spared myself the blow which has fallen on you, I can form some conception of what it must have been

* W. F. Monypenny and G. E. Buckle, *The Life of Benjamin Disraeli* (new edition in 2 vols., New York: Macmillan, 1929), Vol. II, pp. 563, 564, 569, 570, 572, and 1486.

and be. I do not presume to offer you the consolation which you will seek from another and higher quarter. I offer only the assurance which all who know you, all who knew Lady Beaconsfield, and especially those among them who like myself enjoyed for a length of time her marked though unmerited regard, may perhaps render without impropriety; the assurance that in this trying hour they feel deeply for you, and with you. . . .

To William Ewart Gladstone

Hughenden Manor, Jan. 24, 1873.—I am much touched by your kind words in my great sorrow. I trust, I earnestly trust, that you may be spared a similar affliction. Marriage is the greatest earthly happiness, when founded on complete sympathy. That hallowed lot was mine, and for a moiety of my existence; and I know it is yours.

Among Lady Beaconsfield's papers was found a touching letter of farewell to her husband, written many years before, in view of the high probability that she, who was the elder by twelve years, would be the first to die.

June 6, 1856.
My own Dear Husband,—If I should depart this life before you, leave orders that we may be buried in the same grave at whatever distance you may die from England. And now, God bless you, my kindest, dearest! You have been a perfect husband to me. Be put by my side in the same grave. And now, farewell, my dear Dizzy. Do not live alone, dearest. Some one I earnestly hope you may find as attached to you as your own devoted Mary Anne.

From Queen Victoria

Windsor Castle, Dec. 15, 1872.—The Queen well knows that Mr. Disraeli will *not* consider the expression of her heartfelt sympathy an intrusion in this his first hour of desolation and overwhelming grief, and therefore she at once attempts to express what she feels. The Queen knew and admired as well as appreciated the unbounded devotion and affection which united him to the dear partner of his life, whose only thought was him.

And therefore the Queen knows also *what* Mr. Disraeli has lost and what he must suffer. The only consolation to be found is in *her* present peace and freedom from suffering, in the recollection of their life of happiness and in the blessed certainty of eternal reunion.

May God support and sustain him is the Queen's sincere prayer.

Her children are all anxious to express their sympathy. *Yesterday* was the anniversary of her great loss.

The Queen and Mr. Disraeli*

In 1868 Disraeli and his Conservative cabinet resigned. At that time Disraeli wrote to Queen Victoria, demanding a favor for his wife (originally Mrs. Wyndham Lewis, née Evans), whom he married in 1839 and with whom he lived in great and lasting happiness until her death in 1872, though she was twelve years older than he. He dedicated Sybil *to "a perfect wife."*

To Queen Victoria

Nov. 23, 1868.—Mr. Disraeli with his humble duty to your Majesty. Pursuant to your Majesty's gracious intimation he will endeavour to succinctly state what passed in audience with reference to the condition of the Conservative party after the General Election and his personal relations to it.

It was to be considered, 1st, whether it was for your Majesty's comfort and advantage to keep the party together—and, 2ndly, whether if kept together it was expedient that Mr. Disraeli should continue to attempt the task or leave the effort to younger hands. It seemed desirable that the party should be kept together because, although not numerically stronger, its moral influence appeared to be increased from the remarkably popular elements of which the Conservative party was now formed under the influence of the new Reform Act. Viewing England only, the Conservative party in the House of Commons will represent the majority of the population of that country.

This is a strange and most unforeseen result. It did not appear after great deliberation that any person could guide this party for your Majesty's comfort and welfare with the same advantage as Mr. Disraeli, as no one could be so intimately acquainted with your Majesty's wishes and objects as himself. . . .

* W. F. Monypenny and G. E. Buckle, *The Life of Benjamin Disraeli* (new edition in 2 volumes; New York: Macmillan, 1929), Vol. II, pp. 438, 439, 440, and 569.

Mr. Disraeli might say that at his time of life and with the present prospects, it is a dreary career again to lead and form an Opposition party: but he does not say so, because in truth, if in that post he could really serve your Majesty and your Majesty really felt that, it would be a sufficient object and excitement in public life, and he should be quite content even if he were never Minister again.

But next to your Majesty there is one to whom he owes everything, and who has looked forward to this period of their long united lives as one of comparative repose and of recognised honor. Might Mr. Disraeli therefore, after 31 years of Parliamentary toil, and after having served your Majesty on more than one occasion, if not with prolonged success at least with unfaltering devotion, humbly solicit your Majesty to grant those honors to his wife which perhaps under ordinary circumstances your Majesty would have deigned to bestow on him?

It would be an entire reward to him, and would give spirit and cheerfulness to the remainder of his public life, when he should be quite content to be your Majesty's servant if not your Majesty's Minister. He would humbly observe that no precedents are necessary for such a course, but there are several. . . .

Mrs. Disraeli has a fortune of her own adequate to any position in which your Majesty might deign to place her. Might her husband then hope that your Majesty would be graciously pleased to create her Viscountess Beaconsfield, a town with which Mr. Disraeli has been long connected and which is the nearest town to his estate in Bucks which is not yet ennobled?

From Queen Victoria

Windsor Castle, Nov. 24, 1868.—The Queen has received Mr. Disraeli's letter, and has much pleasure in complying with his request that she should confer a peerage on Mrs. Disraeli, as a mark of her sense of his services. The Queen thinks that Mr. Disraeli, with whom she will part with much regret, can render her most useful service even when not in office; and she would have been very sorry if he had insisted on retiring from public life.

The Queen can indeed truly sympathise with his devotion to Mrs. Disraeli, who in her turn is so deeply attached to him, and she hopes they met yet enjoy many years of happiness together.

The Queen will gladly confer the title of Viscountess Beaconsfield on Mrs. Disraeli.

The Queen cannot conclude without expressing her deep sense of Mr. Disraeli's great kindness and consideration towards her, not only in what concerned her personally, but in listening to her wishes—which were however always prompted by the sole desire to promote the good of her country.

To Queen Victoria

Nov. 25, 1868.—Mr. Disraeli at your Majesty's feet offers to your Majesty his deep gratitude for your Majesty's inestimable favor and for the terms—so gracious and so graceful—in which your Majesty has deigned to speak of his efforts when working under a Sovereign whom it is really a delight to serve.

From Queen Victoria

Windsor Castle, April 5, 1881.

Dearest Lord Beaconsfield,—I send you a few of your favourite spring flowers—this time from the slopes here. I will send more from Osborne.

I wd. have proposed to come to see you, but I think it is far better you shd. be quite quiet, and that I may then have the great pleasure of coming to see you when we come back from Osborne, wh. won't be long. You are very constantly in my thoughts, and I wish I could do anything to cheer you and be of the slightest use or comfort.

With earnest wishes for your uninterrupted progress in recovery, Ever yours affectionately, V.R.I.

You shall hear of our safe arrival at Osborne as usual.

[*Beaconsfield died on April 19, 1881. The anniversary of his death has been celebrated as Primrose Day, the primrose having supposedly been his favorite flower.*]

Gladstone Before Forming
His Second Ministry*

Gladstone was seventy when, after a successful campaign in Scotland against Disraeli's foreign policy, a general election seemed ahead and the leadership of the Liberal Party and the post of prime minister in case of a Liberal victory was involved. In connection with these problems Gladstone corresponded with John Bright and Lord Wolverton.

To Mr. Bright

Nov. 28, 1879.—You will probably recollect that during your last visit to Hawarden you suggested to me in a walk the expectation or the possibility that when the return of liberals to power seemed probable, there might be a popular call for my resuming the leadership of the party, and that I stated to you what I believed, and you I think admitted, to be the reasons against it. These, if I remember right, were four, and I attached to them differing degrees of weight.

The first was that my health and strength would be unequal to the strain at my time of life.

The second, that the work to be done was so formidable that hardly any amount of courage availed to look it in the face.

The third, weightier than these, was that a liberal government under me would be the object from the first of an amount and kind of hostility, such as materially to prejudice its acts and weaken or, in given circumstances, neutralise its power for good.

The fourth, that I was absolutely precluded under present circumstances, being bound by the clearest considerations of honour and duty to render a loyal allegiance to Granville as leader of the party, and to Hartington as leader in the Commons, and

* John Morley, *The Life of William Ewart Gladstone* (New York: The Macmillan Company, 1903), Vol. II, pp. 599-603.

was entirely disabled from so much as entertaining any proposition that could directly or indirectly tend to their displacement.

There is a fifth consideration that now presses me, of which the grounds had hardly emerged in regard to myself personally at the time when we conversed together. Nothing could be so painful, I may almost say so odious to me, as to force myself, or to be forced, upon the Queen, under circumstances where the choice of another from the ranks of the same party would save her from being placed in a difficulty of that peculiar kind. This, it may be said, belongs to the same category as my first and second objections; but there it is.

The enthusiasm of Scotland is something wonderful. As to the county of Midlothian, I doubt whether the well-informed tories themselves in the least expect to win. We go to Taymouth on Monday. I hope you are well and hearty and see cause to be contented with the progress of opinion. The more I think about the matter, the more strange and mysterious does it seem to me that any party in this free nation should be found to sanction and uphold policy and proceedings like those of the last two years in particular. I have written this because I am desirous you should have clearly before you the matter of my conversation with you, and the means of verifying it.

Mr. Bright to Mr. Gladstone

Rochdale, Dec. 12, 1879.—Perhaps I ought to have written to you sooner to acknowledge the receipt of your letter of the 28th ult., but I preferred to let you get home before I wrote, and I was in truth rather puzzled as to what I ought to say.

You, with sufficient accuracy, describe the purport of your remarks during our conversation when I was with you a year ago. I saw the difficulty, then in the future, now perhaps near upon us. But it is one in which nothing can be done, and 'a masterly inactivity' seems the only wise course. If a break-up of the present concern comes, the Queen will be advised to send for Granville or Hartington. The one sent for will accept and attempt to form a government, or he may have grave doubts, and say that you are the only man, etc.; he will consult the other, and will consult you. Meantime there may be a 'pronouncement' on the part of the people, through the press and public meetings, which will have a sudden effect on negotiations and on the views of the Queen, and may decide the question. If such a time should come, then you will have to say what is possible, and I hope you will be able to decide rightly, and with reference solely to the interests of the country and the service you owe to the crown as representing the nation. You will act with a most strict honour to Granville and Hartington, as I believe they will act to you. If, as I hope for and believe, no selfish ambition will come in to make mischief, the question will be determined in such a manner as to content all honest men, and what is best for all will be done. I am often asked as to the future. I reply only so as to say nothing to add to the evident difficulty of the situation.

Your Scotch expedition has been one of discovery and of conquest. The tory press and partizans are evidently astonished at it. The government speakers have no new defence, and they want the past to be forgotten. Mr. Smith, first lord, I see, entirely rejoices in what has been done in South Africa, though 'a few lives' have been lost by it. This official life seems sorely to demoralise some homely and decent people. I am fairly well so far during the winter, but I seem feeble when I compare myself with your activity and power. . . . We are to have meetings in Birmingham during January. I should prefer the quiet of obscurity to these meetings. I hope Mrs. Gladstone and your daughter have enjoyed their Scotch trip and are well after it.

Five days later came Lord Wolverton's report of the state of feeling on these delicate topics in high places in London. He had seen Lord Granville on the evening of the 16th:—

To most affectionate inquiries as to your health and powers, I gave a most satisfactory account, and the conversation then went to the question as to the effect which your recent triumphant progress in Midlothian and the North had produced upon your mind. I frankly said that you had in my opinion not anticipated such a marked expression of public feeling, and that it had doubtless tended to lead your mind to the consideration of the position of the party, and to the fact that public opinion might call upon you to an extent which no one could have looked for. I then (with anxiety to convey what I know to be your desire) most earnestly impressed upon Lord Granville that you had upon every occasion when the subject was alluded to, prefaced all you had to say with the strongest expressions of loyalty to Hartington and himself. That I felt convinced that nothing would induce you to encourage, or to even listen to, any attempt which others might make to disturb the existing state of things as to the leadership, unless the wish was very clearly expressed to you by Hartington and himself, and you would demand full proof that their interests and that of the party strongly pointed to the reconsideration of your own position. I need hardly say that, though I felt it my duty to take care that I did not understate your feelings, it was not necessary to reassure Granville upon that point.

The conversation then went to the state of the party and its present position. I learnt that a private meeting had been held at Devonshire House in the morning. I believe Hartington, Granville, Cardwell, Adam, and Harcourt were present. My *impression* is that the advice Adam gave as to the elections, was that 'union in the party at this moment would not be promoted by a change of front.' I do not mean to say that the question of leadership was *actually discussed,* but I *suspect* the conversation was turned somewhat upon the point which you place 'third' in your letter to Bright. To sum it all up, I do not think you will at present be troubled by any application to you from Granville and Hartington.

The third point in the letter to Mr. Bright was the question whether a liberal government under Mr. Gladstone would not be exposed to a special degree of hostility, due to the peculiar antagonism that his personality excited. In a later letter (December 20), Wolverton tells Mr. Gladstone that in the conversation of the 16th, "Lord Granville raised the point you made your third in your note to Bright, and that he did converse upon at some length, *evidently having real fears that many of our weak-kneed ones would feel some alarm if Hartington went from the front* now, *and that the tories would intensify this to the uttermost. I think this was all." Another sentence indicates Lord Wolverton's own view:—*

"Lord Granville is not sanguine as to the future. As you know, he is always inclined to 'temporise'; this is his line now, and he is perhaps right. You know my fear was that without your name in front, the battle at the election would be fought at a great disadvantage. But I see the immense difficulty of a change of front *now*, even if they desired it and you consented to it. This you also feel, I know."

To all this Mr. Gladstone replied to Wolverton as follows:—

Hawarden, December 18, 1879.—I thank you much for your letter. What you report yourself to have said is quite satisfactory to me. If Granville said more than you had mentioned, anything that fell from him would be acceptable to me. When I saw your envelope, I felt a dread lest the contents should be more substantive; a relief came on reading them. But these communications are useful, as they give distinctness to ideas, and through ideas to intentions. I may state mine as follows: 1. My ears are shut against all the world, except it were Granville and Hartington. 2. And even to them unless they spoke together, and in clear and decisive language. 3. They are the judges whether to speak, as well as when to speak. But as an individual, I am of opinion that there is not a case for their speaking now. 4. Were they to speak now, and as I have defined above, I should then say let us have nothing more than a formula, and let the substance of it be that by the nature of things no man in my position could make beforehand an absolute renunciation, and that the leadership in the next parliament must, like everything else, be considered in connection with what may appear at the dissolution to be the sense of the country, but that my action individually has been and will continue to be that of a follower of Lord Granville and Lord Hartington. One thing I would ask of you as a fast friend. If you think that in anything I fall short by omission or commission of perfect loyalty as a member of the party, I beg you to tell me.

Act for the Better Government of India*

On the termination of the Indian Mutiny of 1857 the British Crown assumed the government of India. On November 1, 1858, a royal proclamation was read at the Durbar in Allahabad announcing Queen Victoria's principles for the future government of India.

Whereas, for divers weighty reasons, we have resolved, by and with the advice and consent of the lords spiritual and temporal and commons, in Parliament assembled, to take upon ourselves the government of the territories in India, heretofore administered in trust for us by the Honorable East India Company.

Now, therefore, we do by these presents notify and declare that, by the advice and consent aforesaid, we have taken upon ourselves the said government; and we hereby call upon all our subjects within the said territories to be faithful, and to bear true allegiance to us, our heirs and successors, and to submit themselves to the authority of those whom we may hereafter from time to time see fit to appoint to administer the government of our said territories in our name and on our behalf.

We hereby announce to the native princes of India, that all treaties and engagements made with them by or under the authority of the Honorable East India Company are by us accepted, and will be scrupulously maintained, and we look for the like observance on their part.

We desire no extension of our present territorial possessions; and, while we will permit no aggression upon our dominions or our rights to be attempted with impunity, we shall sanction no encroachment on those of others. We shall respect the rights, dignity, and honour of native princes as our own; and we desire that they, as well as our own subjects, should enjoy that pros-

* Royal Proclamation of November 1, 1858.

perity and that social advancement which can only be secured by internal peace and good government.

We hold ourselves bound to the natives of our Indian territories by the same obligations of duty which bind us to our other subjects, and those obligations, by the blessing of Almighty God, we shall faithfully and conscientiously fulfill.

Firmly relying ourselves on the truth of Christianity, and acknowledging with gratitude the solace of religion, we disclaim alike the right and the desire to impose our convictions on any of our subjects. We declare it to be our royal will and pleasure that none be in anywise favoured, none molested or disquieted, by reason of their religious faith or observances, but that all shall alike enjoy the equal and impartial protection of the law; and we do strictly charge and enjoin all those who may be in authority under us that they abstain from all interference with the religious belief or worship of any of our subjects on pain of our highest displeasure.

And it is our further will that, as far as may be, our subjects, of whatever race or creed, be freely and impartially admitted to offices in our service, the duties of which they may be qualified by their education, ability, and integrity, duly to discharge. . . .

Our clemency will be extended to all offenders, save and except those who have been or shall be convicted of having directly taken part in the murder of British subjects. With regard to such the demands of justice forbid the exercise of mercy.

To those who have willingly given asylum to murderers, knowing them to be such, or who may have acted as leaders or instigators in revolt, their lives alone can be guaranteed; but in apportioning the penalty due to such persons, full consideration will be given to the circumstances under which they have been induced to throw off their allegiance; and large indulgence will be shown to those whose crimes may appear to have originated in too credulous acceptance of the false reports circulated by designing men.

To all others in arms against the government we hereby promise unconditional pardon, amnesty, and oblivion of all offenses against ourselves, our crown and dignity, on the return to their homes and peaceful pursuits.

The Intent of British Imperialism*

On January 1, 1877, Queen Victoria was proclaimed Empress of India. On the same day The (*London*) Times *expressed in an editorial the sentiments guiding British imperialism.*

Often to-day will England turn her eyes towards that far East with which her destinies have been so mysteriously associated. At the length of one continent she sees an Empire writhing in what may be its last agony; near the length of another she sees the inauguration of a new Empire, and that her own. That the former of these Empires should have been menaced by hostile ambition, by suicidal folly, and by prophecy which ever dogs the steps of doom, now for four centuries is not a matter of surprise. But India, which has quietly dropped into our waiting rather than expectant hands, has been the supreme object of human desire during all the ages of which we have the slightest knowledge. An invasion of the people beyond the Indus sufficiently successful to allow of a return was the crowning achievement of gods, demigods, and heroes. The Macedonian conqueror just saved his soldiers and his name by stopping on the threshhold of the coveted dominion. His successors made conquests on the banks of the Indus and its tributaries, and they even founded a kingdom, but it had disappeared before the Christian era. The Romans were content to maintain friendly relations with the border States of India and called it giving laws to a willing people. But from that day to this no Power, however numerous, however enterprising, able, and unscrupulous, has ever done more than surprise and reduce large portions of the Peninsula, and hold them for a time by sheer force of arms. The annals of India are little else than a succession of unprovoked conquests, maintained by terror, and without the arts of policy and peace, by which alone different

* *The Times* (London), January 1, 1877.

races can be brought to a lasting unity. Here and there a green spot of common human benevolence reveals itself in the dreary retrospect, and India has thereby learnt to dream of rulers better than the cruel and licentious conceptions of her own mythology. But rarely indeed has there been any trace of that true Imperial instinct which conquers to conciliate, which chastises in kindness, which comforts the weak, tames the strong, and makes it a rule that the triumphs of peace shall adorn or hide those of war. It might be that not only national genius but national opportunities were necessary for the exercise of such salutary and creative beneficence. It cannot be denied that England has both the opportunities and the genius to use them. Since the days of Rome no Power has so combined the gifts of war and of peace, of policy, of material improvement, and of enterprise by sea and land, and, above all, the art of dealing with discordant races, as our own. When the Roman poet conjured up in his prophetic fancy a temple, and games, and a theatre, for the glory and worship of Augustus, triumphant over the East, he saw in ivory and gold upon the temple gates the Nile surging with flood and war, Asia conquered, and the Ganges witnessing the subjugation of her sons. But we, too, of this remote island had a place in that vision. Gigantic Britons, posted on either side, seemed to draw the tapestry that revealed that ever-changing scene. Little did the poet think that these very Britons would one day raise the curtain and show such a scene as that of this day.

It cannot but be with a conflict of hopes and fears that we witness an achievement so long desired, and so often attempted, either wholly in vain or with a success so partial and short-lived that England would deem it hardly worth the sacrifice. That distrust has shown itself in the repeated unwillingness of this country to accept the dignity it had justly earned till forced upon it by the necessity of the case. In the midst of the day's triumph there will rise up the memories of those who grasped India only to let her fall from their hands. We will dispel the thought that their fate may be ours. It can hardly be to share the rapid vicissitudes of Asia, and to prove that policy is the creature of accident, that we have entered that new sphere. It is rather that we may introduce into it the deeper sentiments and grander ideas that have made Europe hitherto the leading quarter of the world. India, in itself, never had the prospect or even the thought of a political unity. Like Africa, the region was peopled with numberless races, who had their quarrels, but who were apparently capable of no grander objects than could be attained within their own territories, which were sufficient for the population. The very notion of a larger unity must have been imported by the Mahomedans, who, after many lesser inroads and menaces, broke through the North-Western passes into the Valley of the Ganges and its tributaries, two generations before our own Norman Conquest. The power and the opportunities at the command of Mahmoud and his successors were beyond all comparison greater than those of our Norman Kings, but there was this fatal difference—that, whereas the latter brought with them a sublime faith, a rational policy, and a matured system, and thereby threw the Saxon into a mould far better than his own, the Mahomedans of Ghizni were never anything else than soldiers, robbers, and plunderers, intent on rapine, greedy of spoil, and looking to sensual enjoyment and empty show as the proper fruits of war. Holding the mountain passes, they could easily overrun, again and again, the vast plains spread before that region, whether to the North or to the South; nor did the people they had conquered, and had to reconquer again and again, make the slightest advance to a more than dynastic union, or to common institutions. After two centuries of continual war, an Afghan dynasty ruled in Delhi as the capital of its Indian possessions, making expeditions to the West, and far to the North-West, and even to Central Asia, but giving very little trouble apparently to Southern and Eastern India. After a century, that dynasty gave place to another, and by this time the Mahomedans founded a new and separate kingdom on the western coast, never extending far into the interior. Like every other formation up to that time known in India, this last very speedily split into several smaller sovereignties. Let our readers glance over the survey of Indian History we publish in our Outer Sheet this morning, and they will see that four hundred years ago India was in the same anarchy it had ever been.

It was in such a state of things that the Empire of the Great Mogul was founded about the date of our Reformation, with its seat at Delhi. It never comprised the whole peninsula, or even attempted more than raids into the territories of independent States, being sufficiently occupied in protecting its own territory from predatory races such as the Sikhs in one direction and the Mahrattas in another. It existed as a military power and kept its ground by movement; but, in truth, it dissolved faster than it formed, for the seeds of dissolution were in its very birth. It cast off limb after limb, and the Powers, or rather the nominal representatives of old Powers, that appear to-day on the plains of Delhi to present their homage to the British Empress of India are the fragments of that Mogul Empire which ceased to have more than a nominal existence about a century ago. The very titles that impose upon our imagination signify nothing but various kinds of personal service to the Great Mogul, whose throne was founded not a century before the appearance of the English in India. When Nadir Shah marched upon Delhi he encountered only the feeble head, or rather the mutilated trunk, of the shattered Empire. It had long existed only on its old glories, incapable of good, and therefore full of harm. A nominal head is worse than no head at all, because it becomes the sanction of universal disorder. The magnificent personages whom our Delhi dispatch of this morning chronicles as having pitched their camps round the camp of the British Viceroy, exchanging visits with him, and prepared to accept the Empress Victoria, as the rightful occupant of the forfeited throne of the Great Mogul, have no small claims of our consideration. They stand, indeed, for many millions, and for vast and fertile countries. Their truest dignity is that which they have received from British recognition. We must not inquire overmuch into the histories of their dynasties and of their realms. We must not even suppose that they represent policies or administrations in our sense of the words. We must not pry too closely into their own lives if they are no longer children, as some of them happily are. There are too many dragons of virtue at home to make this a safe question. Politically they represent altogether one great fact, which is the single-all-sufficient justification of this day's ceremony. They represent the proved impossibility of India uniting herself by her own internal development, or by any Asiatic agency. A self-made Indian union is as much an impossibility as a self-made African union. But we have only to recall the terrible catastrophes of which Delhi has been the scene, and which were but samples of Indian history, to see how needful union is to the two hundred and fifty millions in that peninsula. Disunion and even anarchy might be bearable in times when the population was a fifth of that we have now to deal with. They now mean famine, internecine wars for mere subsistence, and calamities beyond even Indian precedent. It is true that order and peace themselves are the source of a new difficulty. A strange but not altogether ill-founded instinct makes the people of India love and worship most the memories of the great destroyers. War diminishes the survivors, but not in the same degree that which they have to share, and therefore does not affect exclusively in one direction the struggle for subsistence. Peace multiplies indefinitely the competitors for the diminishing supply. It is a sixth part of the human race, so it has been calculated, that our Correspondent at the Imperial Assemblage has to record as marshalled by representation to-day before the Empress Victoria's flag to hear the proclamation of the title she has won and the allegiance they are bound to. Providence, so we are proud to say, has cast them upon our care. They are become our children. How shall we feed so many? How shall we double or treble the productiveness of the peninsula, which, between seas and impassable mountains, is hardly less an island than our own? How shall we save them from worse famine—the superstitions that enslave and degrade them? These are questions that will present themselves to-day, and which have long been clamorous for a reply.

Ottoman Reforms*

At the end of the Crimean War, on February 18, 1856, Sultan Abdul Medjid (1839-1861) inaugurated the era of the Westernization of the Ottoman Empire by the Imperial Decree, the Hatt-i-Humayoun. Its principle passages read:

All the Privileges and Spiritual Immunities granted by my ancestors *ab antiquo,* and at subsequent dates, to all Christian communities or other non-Mussulman persuasions established in my Empire under my protection shall be confirmed and maintained.

Every Christian or other non-Mussulman community shall be bound within a fixed period, and with the concurrence of a Commission composed *ad hoc* of members of its own body, to proceed with my high approbation and under the inspection of my Sublime Porte, to examine into its actual Immunities and Privileges, and to discuss and submit to my Sublime Porte the Reforms required by the progress of civilization and of the age. The powers conceded to the Christian Patriarchs and Bishops by the Sultan Mahomet II and his successors, shall be made to harmonize with the new position which my generous and beneficient intentions insure to these communities. . . . The principles of nominating the Patriarchs for life, after the revision of the rules of election now in force, shall be exactly carried out, conformably to the tenor of the Firmans of Investiture. . . . The ecclesiastical dues, of whatever sort or nature they be, shall be abolished and replaced by fixed revenues of the Patriarchs and heads of communities. . . . In the towns, small boroughs, and villages, where the whole population is of the same Religion, no obstacle shall be offered to the repair, ac-

* E. Hertslet *The Map of Europe by Treaty* (London: Butterworth & Co., 1875-1891), Vol. II, pp. 1243-1249.

cording to their original plan, of buildings set apart for Religious Worship, for Schools, for Hospitals, and for Cemeteries. . . .

Every distinction or designation tending to make any class whatever of the subjects of my Empire inferior to another class, on account of their Religion, Language, or Race, shall be for ever effaced from the Administrative Protocol. The laws shall be put in force against the use of any injurious or offensive term, either among private individuals or on the part of the authorities.

As all forms of Religion are and shall be freely professed in my dominions, no subject of my Empire shall be hindered in the exercise of the Religion that he professes. . . . No one shall be compelled to change their Religion . . . and . . . all the subjects of my Empire, without distinction of nationality, shall be admissible to public employments. . . . All the subjects of my Empire, without distinction of nationality, shall be admissible to public employments. . . . All the subjects of my Empire, without distinction, shall be received into the Civil and Military Schools of the Government. . . . Moreover, every community is authorized to establish Public Schools of Science, Art, and Industry. . . .

All Commerical, Correctional, and Criminal Suits between Mussulmans and Christian or other non-Mussulmans of different sects, shall be referred to Mixed Tribunals. The proceedings of these Tribunals shall be public: the parties shall be confronted, and shall produce their witnesses, whose testimony shall be received, without distinction, upon oath taken according to the religious law of each sect. . . .

Penal, Correctional, and Commercial Laws, and Rules of Procedure for the Mixed Tribunals, shall be drawn up as soon as possible, and formed into a code. . . . Proceedings shall be taken, for the reform of the Penitentiary System. . . .

The organization of the Police . . . shall be revised in such a manner as to give to all the peaceable subjects of my Empire the strongest guarantees for the safety both of their persons and property. . . . Christian subjects, and those of other non-Mussulman sects, . . . shall, as well as Mussulmans, be subject to the obligations of the Law of Recruitment. The principles of nominating the Patriarchs for life, after the revision of the rules of election now in force, shall be exactly carried out, conformably to the tenor of the Firmans of Investiture. . . . The ecclesiastical dues, of whatever sort or nature they be, shall be abolished and replaced by fixed revenues of the Patriarchs and heads of communities. . . . In the towns, small boroughs, and villages, where the whole population is of the same Religion, no obstacle shall be offered to the repair, according to their original plan, of buildings set apart for Religious Worship, for Schools, for Hospitals, and for Cemeteries. . . .

Proceedings shall be taken for a Reform in the Constitution of the Provincial and Communal Councils, in order to ensure fairness in the choice of the Deputies of the Mussulman, Christian, and other communities, and freedom of voting in the Councils. . . .

As the Laws regulating the purchase, sale, and disposal of Real Property are common to all the subjects of my Empire, it shall be lawful for Foreigners to possess Landed Property in my dominions. . . .

The Taxes are to be levied under the same denomination from all the subjects of my Empire, without distinction of class or of Religion. The most prompt and energetic means for remedying the abuses in collecting the Taxes, and especially the Tithes, shall be considered. The system of direct collection shall gradually, and as soon as possible, be substituted for the plan of Farming, in all the branches of the Revenues of the State.

A special Law having been already passed, which declared that the Budget of the Revenue and Expenditure of the State shall be drawn up and made known every year, the said law shall be most scrupulously observed. . . .

The heads of each Community and a Delegate, designated by my Sublime Porte, shall be summoned to take part in the deliberations of the Supreme Council of Justice on all occasions which might interest the generality of the subjects of my Empire. . . .

Steps shall be taken for the formation of Banks and other similar institutions, so as to effect a reform in the monetary and financial system, as well as to create Funds to be employed in augmenting the sources of the material wealth of my Empire.

Steps shall also be taken for the formation of Roads and Canals to increase the facilities of communication and increase the sources of the wealth of the country. Everything that can impede commerce or agriculture shall be abolished. . . .

Danilevsky: Pan-Slavism*

In his book Russia and Europe: An Inquiry into the Cultural and Political Relations of the Slav World and of the German-Latin World *(1869), Nikolai Danilevsky (1822-85) stated the incompatibility of Slav civilization with Western civilization, the great superiority of the former and its victory in the inevitable struggle between the two. For that purpose the Russians, the foremost Slav power, had to liberate and to unite all the Slavs and to conquer Constantinople and the (Middle) East.*

In the preceding chapters, strictly speaking, I finished my self-appointed task. A special case—the course of the Schleswig-Holstein question as compared with the (Middle) Eastern question before the Crimean War—gave me the opportunity to discuss the hostility of Europe towards Russia and the Slav world. . . . This investigation led me to the conclusion that this hostility lies in the deep gulf separating the world of the Slavs and the Germano-Roman world—a gulf which reaches down to the very origins of the general stream of universal history.

I attempted to develop this theoretical approach and to supplement it with indications about the main differences between the Slavs and the Germano-Roman cultural-historical types, and about the fatal predicament to which this Westernization or Europeanization has led us, and the extent to which it is the cause of the disease from which Russia's social body suffers, a disease which is the source of all our social ills. Only historical events can remedy this disease and raise the spirit of our society, suffering from spiritual decay and abasement. The cure is possible and probable, because so far the disease has luckily penetrated only the surface of the social structure. We can see an event, or rather a whole series of events, endowed with a

* Hans Kohn, *The Mind of Modern Russia* (New York: Harper Torchbooks, 1962), pp. 195-210.

healthy dynamism, in the latest phase of the struggle known as the (Middle) Eastern question, whose origins are rooted in the general course of universal historical development. This struggle must shortly stamp its imprint upon an entire historical period. The importance of this inevitably approaching struggle forces us to try to understand the objections raised against the only decision useful to the Slav world—the full political liberation of all the Slav peoples and the formation of a Pan-Slav union under the hegemony of Russia. The Pan-Slav union will guarantee our success in this struggle.

Religious truth, in the eternal form of Christianity, was discovered and adopted with humility and exaltation by new peoples, who were rich in gifts of spiritual nature, among which one has to include ardent religious feelings. In this same religious doctrine there was, as its central tenet, the need to do away with slavery; and in reality, slavery appeared only as a transitory phase in the life of the Germano-Roman peoples. These peoples also revealed themselves richly endowed with political sense and an ability for cultural development: scientific, artistic, and industrial. They were not fated, however, to have these great gifts fully realized, due to the violence of their character. With them Roman love for power and Roman state structure fell upon a receptive soil. In this way, Christian truth was distorted, and the Church was transformed into the religiously political despotism of Catholicism. This church despotism in conjunction with feudal despotism, which took root in the violence of the German character, and with the despotism of scholasticism, which had taken its origin in a slavish attitude to the forms of ancient science, oriented all the history of Europe towards a severe struggle, ending in a three-fold anarchy. It comprised a religious anarchy, that is, Protestantism with the idea of basing religious truth upon personal authority; a philosophical anarchy, or an all-embracing skeptical materialism, which began to take on the character of a faith and little by little replaced religious conviction; and a socio-political anarchy, a contradiction between an ever growing political democratism and economic feudalism. As these anarchies are substantially the forerunners and instruments of decay, they cannot, of course, be considered viable investments in the treasury of mankind; and the Germano-Roman cultural-historical type cannot be considered a successful representative of the religious, or of the socio-economic aspect of cultural activity. . . .

On the other hand, . . . from an objective, factual viewpoint, the Russians and the majority of Slav peoples became, with the Greeks, the chief guardians of the living tradition of religious truth, Orthodoxy, and in this way they continued the high calling, which was the destiny of Israel and Byzantium: to be the chosen people. . . .

Whatever the future may bring we are entitled, on the evidence of the past alone, to consider the Slavs among the most gifted families of the human race in political ability. Here we may turn our attention to the special character of this political ability and show how it manifested itself during the growth of the Russian state. The Russians do not send out colonists to create new political societies, as the Greeks did in antiquity or the English in modern times. Russia does not have colonial possessions, like Rome or like England. The Russian state from early Muscovite times on has been Russia herself, gradually, irresistibly spreading on all sides, settling neighboring nonsettled territories, and assimilating into herself and into her national boundaries foreign populations. This basic character of Russian expansion was misunderstood because of the distortion of the original Russian point of view through Europeanization, the origin of every evil in Russia. . . .

In the socio-economic sphere, Russia is the only large state which has solid ground under its feet, in which there are no landless masses, and in which, consequently, the social edifice does not rest on the misery of the majority of the citizens and on the insecurity of their situation. In Russia, only, there cannot and does not exist any contradiction between political and economic ideals. This contradiction threatens disaster to European life. . . . The factors that give such superiority to the Russian social structure over the European, and give it an unshakeable stability, are the peasants' land and its common ownership. On this health of Russia's socio-economic structure we found our hope for the great socio-economic significance of the Slav cultural-historical type. This type has been able for the first time to create a just and normal system of human activity, which embraces not only human relations in the moral and political sphere, but also man's mastery of nature, which is a means of satisfying human needs and requirements. Thus it establishes not only formal equality in the relations between citizens, but a real and concrete equality. . . .

The political independence of the race is the indispensable foundation of culture, and consequently all the Slav forces must be directed towards this goal. Independence is indispensable in two respects; without the consciousness of Slav racial unity, as distinct from other races, an independent culture is impossible; and without fruitful interaction between the Slav peoples, liberated from foreign powers and from their national divisions, diversity and richness of culture are impossible. A well-known example of the beneficial influence of unity is the relationship and interaction between the spiritual developments of Great Russia and the Ukraine.

The requisite preliminary achievement of political independence has still another importance in the cultural as well as in all other spheres: the struggle against the Germano-Roman world (without which Slav independence is impossible) will help to eradicate the cancer of imitativeness and the servile attitude towards the West, which through unfavorable conditions has eaten its way into the Slav body and soul. Only now has the historical moment for this cultural development arrived: only with the emanicipation of the peasantry can the period of Russian cultural life begin, and her purely state period of life (which consisted in leading the people from tribal will to civil liberty) end. But first, as a *sine qua non* condition of success, strong and powerful Russia has to face the difficult task of liberating her racial brothers; for this struggle she must steel them and herself in the spirit of independence and Pan-Slav maintain the fundamental hope that the Slav cultural-historical consciousness.

Thus, on the basis of our analysis of the preceding cultural-historical types and of the peculiarities of the Slav world, we can type will, for the first time in history, accomplish a synthesis of all aspects of cultural activity—aspects which were elaborated by its precursors on the historical scene, either in isolation or in incomplete union. We may hope that the Slav type will be the first to embody all four basic cultural activities, the religious, the political, the esthetic-scientific, and the socio-economic. . . .

The Alliance of Austria-Hungary with Germany*

After his retirement from office, Prince Otto von Bismarck wrote his memoirs in which he explained and justified his policy. In the following excerpts he begins with the events of the late summer of 1879.

When Emperor William went to Alexandrovo (Sept. 3), I had already made arrangements at Gastein for a meeting with Count Andrássy, which took place on August 27-28. When I had explained the situation to him he drew therefrom the following conclusion: To a Russo-French alliance the natural counterpoise is an Austro-German alliance. I answered that he had formulated the question to discuss which I had suggested our meeting, and we came readily to a preliminary understanding for a merely defensive alliance against a Russian attack on one of the two sides; but my proposition to extend the alliance to other than Russian attacks, found no favour with the Count. . . .

Before my departure from Gastein I addressed (Sept. 10) the following letter to the King of Bavaria:

> Your Majesty was so gracious on a former occasion as to express your most exalted satisfaction with the efforts which I directed to the object of securing for the German Empire peace and friendship with both her great neighbors, Austria and Russia alike. In the course of the last three years this problem has increased in difficulty, as Russian policy has come to be entirely dominated by the partly warlike tendencies of Panslavism. . . . The leading minister, in so far as such a minister there is at present in Russia, is the War Minister, Milutin. At his demand the peace, in which Russia is threatened by no one, has yet been followed by the mighty preparations which . . . have raised . . . the footing of the army of the West, which is kept ready for active

* Bismarck, *Reflections and Reminiscences* (Leipzig: Tauchnitz, 1899), Vol. III, pp. 180-184, 197-198, 201-202.

service, by about 400,000 men. These preparations can only be intended as a menace to Austria or Germany, and the military establishments in the kingdom of Poland correspond to such a design. The War Minister has also . . . unreservedly declared that Russia must prepare for a war "with Europe."

If it is indubitable that Czar Alexander, without desiring the war with Turkey, nevertheless waged it under stress of Panslavist influence, in consequence of the greater and more dangerous impression which the agitation at the back of it now makes on the mind of the Czar, we may readily apprehend that it may also succeed in obtaining Czar Alexander's sanction for further warlike enterprises on the western frontier. . . .

Austria regards the restless Russian policy with as much disquietude as we, and seems to be inclined, for an understanding with us for common defence against a possible Russian attack on either of the two Powers.

If the German Empire were to come to such an understanding with Austria, an understanding which should have in view the cultivation of peace with Russia as sedulously as before, but should also provide for joint defence in the event of an attack by her upon either of the allied powers, I should see in it an essential security for the peace of Europe. Thus mutually assured, both empires might continue their efforts for the further consolidation of the Three Emperors' Alliance. The German Empire in alliance with Austria would not lack the support of England, and the peace of Europe, the common interest of both empires, would be guaranteed by 2,000,000 fighting men. In this alliance, purely defensive as it would be, there would be nothing to excite jealousy in any quarter: for in the German Confederation the same mutual guarantee subsisted with the sanction of international law for fifty years after 1815. If no such understanding is come to, Austria will not be to blame if, under the influence of Russian threats, and uncertain of the attitude of Germany, she finally seeks an *entente cordiale* with either France or Russia. In the latter case, Germany, by reason of her relation to France, would be in danger of entire isolation on the Continent. Supposing, with France and England, as in 1854, Germany, unless prepared for isolation, would be forced to unite with Russia alone, and, as I fear, to follow in the mistaken and perilous course of Russian domestic and foreign policy.

If Russia compels us to choose between her and Austria, I believe that the disposition which Austria would display towards us would be conservative and peaceable, while that of Russia would be uncertain. . . .

Peace between Germany and Russia may be imperilled by the systematic fomentation of ill-feeling, or by the ambition of Russian or German military men who desire war before they grow too old to distinguish themselves in any other way. The Russian press must needs be characterised by stupidity and disingenuousness in an unusual degree for it to believe and affirm that German policy was determined by aggressive tendencies in concluding the Austrian, and thereafter the Italian, defensive alliance. The disingenuousness was less of Russian than of Polish-French, the stupidity less of Polish-French than of Russian origin. In the field of Russian credulity and ignorance Polisy-French finesse won a victory over that want of finesse in which, according to circumstances, consists now the strength, now the weakness of German policy. In most cases an open and honourable policy succeeds better than the subtlety of earlier ages, but it postulates, if it is to succeed, a degree of personal confidence which can more readily be lost than gained.

The future of Austria, regarded in herself, cannot be reckoned upon with that certainty which is demanded when the conclusion of durable and, so to speak, organic treaties is contemplated. The factors which must be taken into account in this shaping are as manifold as is the mixture of her populations, and to their corrosive and occasionally disruptive force must be added the incalculable influence that the religious element may from time to time, as the power of Rome waxes or wanes, exert upon the directing personalities. Not only Panslavism and the Bulgarian or Bosnian, but also the Serbian, the Roumanian, the Polish, the Czech questions, nay even today the Italian question in the district of Trent, in Trieste, and on the Dalmatian coast, may serve as points of crystallisation not merely for Austrian, but for European crises, by which German interests will be directly affected only in so far as the German Empire enters into a relation of close solidarity with Austria. In Bohemia the antagonism between Germans and Czechs has in some places penetrated so deeply into the army that the officers of the two nationalities in certain regiments hold aloof from one another even to the degree that they will not meet at mess. There is more immediate danger for Germany of becoming involved in grievous and dangerous struggles on her western frontier, by reason of the aggressive, plundering instincts of the French people, which have been greatly developed by her monarchs since the time of Emperor Charles V., in their lust of power at home as well as abroad. . . .

We must and can honourably maintain the alliance with the Austro-Hungarian monarchy; it corresponds to our interests, to the historical traditions of Germany, to the public opinion of our people. The influences and forces under and amid which the future policy of Vienna must be shaped, are, however, more complex than with us, by reason of the manifold diversity of the nationalities, the divergence of their aspirations and activities, the influence of the clergy, and the temptation to which the Danubian countries are exposed in the Balkan and Black Sea latitudes.

We cannot abandon Austria, but neither can we lose sight of the possibility that the policy of Vienna may willy-nilly abandon us. The possibilities which in such a case remain open to us must be clearly realized and steadily borne in mind by German statesmen before the critical moment arrives, nor must their action be determined by prejudice or misunderstanding, but by an entirely dispassionate weighing of the national interests.

William Gladstone:
Europe and War*

In an unsigned article published in the Edinburgh Review *for October 1870, Gladstone foresaw as a consequence of the war the development of a warlike spirit, which dominated the era of 1871-1914 and finally led to the First World War. Gladstone strongly opposed the piling up of huge armaments and huge budgets, a trend of the age.*

We hear much of the civilisation of the Germans. Let them remember, that Italy has been built up, at least from 1860 onwards, upon the groundwork of the expressed desires of the people of its several portions; that England surrendered the possession of the Ionian Islands in deference to the popular desire, expressed through the representative Chamber, to be united to Greece; that even the Emperor Napoleon took Savoy and Nice under cover of a vote, as to which no one can say that it clearly belied the real public sentiment. This is surely a great advance on the old and cruel practice of treating the population of a civilised European country as mere chattels. Are we to revert to that old practice? Will its revival be in harmony with the feeling, the best feeling, of Europe? Will it conduce to future peace? Can Germany afford, and does she mean, to set herself up above European opinion? . . . .

Amidst the many additions which this age has contributed to the comfort and happiness of man, it has made some also to his miseries. And among these last is the deplorable discovery of methods by which we can environ peace with many of the worst attributes of war; as, for instance, with its hostility to the

* The following excerpts are from the article in the *Edinburgh Review,* as reprinted in Gladstone's *Gleanings of Past Years* (London: John Murray, 1879), Vol. IV, pp. 233-257.

regular development of freedom, through the influence of great standing armies, and the prevalence of military ideas; with its hostility to sound and stable government, through crushing taxation, financial embarrassment, and that constant growth of public debt which now, with somewhat rare exceptions, marks the policy of the States of Europe; with the jealous and angry temper, which it kindles between nations; and lastly, with the almost certainty of war itself, as the issue of that state of highly armed preparation, which, we are affectedly told, is the true security for the avoidance of quarrels among men. . . .

In truth the nations of Europe are a family. Some one of them is likely, if not certain, from time to time to be the strongest, either by inherent power or by favouring opportunity. To this strength great influence will attach; and great power over the lot of others. Such influence and power may be abused. In one important respect, Germany may be peculiarly open to temptation to abuse the power which she has undoubtedly acquired. She alone among modern nations has discovered a secret, which releases her from one of the main checks on a disposition to go to war. She has learned to make it pay; to exact from the enemy the cost of her operations in the shape of pecuniary indemnity. . . .

One accomplishment yet remains needful to enable us to hold without envy our free and eminent position. It is that we should do as we would be done by; that we should seek to found a moral empire upon the confidence of the several peoples, not upon their fears, their passions, or their antipathies. Certain it is that a new law of nations is gradually taking hold of the mind, and coming to sway the practice, of the world; a law which recognises independence, which frowns upon aggression, which favours the pacific, not the bloody settlement of disputes, which aims at permanent and not temporary adjustments; above all, which recognises, as a tribunal of paramount authority, the general judgment of civilised mankind. It has censured the aggression of France; it will censure, if need arise, the greed of Germany. "Securus judicat orbis terrarum." It is hard for all nations to go astray. Their ecumenical council sits above the partial passions of those who are misled by interest and disturbed by quarrel. The greatest triumph of our time, a triumph in a region

loftier than that of electricity and steam, will be the enthrone-
ment of this idea of Public Right, as the governing idea of
European policy; as the common and precious inheritance of
all lands, but superior to the passing opinion of any.

Ernest Renan: The Problems of Peace*

After the Franco-Prussian War and the loss of Alsace-Lorraine, Renan wrote a letter, dated September 15, 1871, to his former friend, the German scholar David Friedrich Strauss (1808-1874), who had enthusiastically supported the German war goals.

For the last year I have been in the situation of all those who preach moderation in times of crisis. The evidence and the overwhelming majority of public opinion were against me. But I cannot say that I have been converted. Let us wait for ten or fifteen years. I am convinced that the enlightened part of Germany will then recognize that I was its best friend when I advised gentleness in the use of victory. I do not believe that any extreme solutions will last. I would be much surprised if such an absolute faith in the virtue of a race as that professed by Bismarck and Moltke did not end in discomfiture. By abandoning herself to the statesmen and warriors of Prussia, Germany has mounted a frisky horse which will lead her where she does not wish to go. You play for too high stakes. Your conduct exactly resembles that of France at a period with which one reproaches her most. In 1792 the European powers provoked France; France defeated the powers, which was her right; then she pushed her victory to excesses, in which she was wrong. Excess is bad; pride is the only vice which will be punished in this world. To triumph is always a mistake and in any case something which little befits a philosopher. . . .

It is useless to say that sixty or seventy years ago we acted in the same way, and that we then pillaged, massacred and conquered in Europe. We have always censured these mistakes of the First Empire. They were the work of a generation, with

* Ernest Renan, *La Réforme Intellectuelle et Morale* (Cambridge University Press, 1950).

which we have little in common and whose glory is no longer
ours. If one does not admit a statute of limitations for the violence
of the past, there will be endless war. Lorraine had been part of
the German Empire, without doubt; but Holland, Switzerland,
Italy herself, and if we go back beyond the treaty of Verdun
[843], the whole of France including even Catalonia, formed
part of the German Empire. Alsace today is a German country
by language and race; but before it was invaded by the Germans,
Alsace, like a great portion of southern Germany, was Celtic.
We do not conclude from this fact that southern Germany
ought to be French; but we do not wish to be told that by
ancient right Metz and Luxembourg ought to be German. Nobody could say where this archeology might end. Almost everywhere that the enthusiastic German patriots claim a German
right, we could claim a previous Celtic right. And before the
Celtic period there were Finnish and Laplandish tribes, and
before them the cave dwellers; and before them orang-utans.
With such a philosophy of history there would exist no legitimate
right in the world except that of the orang-utans, who were un-
justly dispossessed by the perfidy of the civilized peoples.

Let us be less absolute: besides the right of the dead, let us
admit a little the right of the living. . . . Europe is a confederation of states united by the common idea of civilization. The
individuality of each nation is constituted without doubt by its
race, its language, its history, its religion, but also by something
much more tangible, by an actual agreement, by the will of the
various provinces of a state to live together. Before the unfortunate annexation of Nice [1860], no part of France wished to
separate herself from France; this was sufficient to make every
dismemberment of France a European crime, though France was
a unity neither in language or race. On the contrary, parts of
Belgium and Switzerland, and to a general degree the Channel
Islands, though they speak French, in no way wish to belong
to France. This is sufficient to make any effort to annex them
by force a criminal act. Alsace is German by language and race,
but she does not wish to belong to the German state; that settles
the question. One speaks of the right of France, of the right of
Germany. These abstractions mean much less to us than the
right of the Alsatians, living human beings, to obey only a power

to which they consent. . . . You have erected in the world a standard of the ethnographical and archeological policy instead of a liberal policy; this policy will be fatal to you. The comparative philology which you have created and which you have wrongly transferred to the political field will bode ill for you.

The Slavs get enthusiastic about it. Every Slav school teacher is becoming your enemy, a termite which ruins your house. How can you believe that the Slavs will not do to you what you are doing to others? The Slav march behind you and follow you step by step. Every affirmation of Germanism is an affirmátion of Slavism. A glance at the affairs of Austria shows that to full evidence. There are twice as many Slavs as Germans. Like the Dragon of the Apocalypse the Slav will one day drag behind him the hordes of Central Asia, the ancient clientele of Genghis Khan and Tamerlane. How much better it would have been for you if you could have reserved for that day the right to appeal to reason, to morality, to friendships based on common principles. Think only how much it will weigh in the balance of the world when one day the Bohemians, the Moravians, the Croatians, the Serbs, all the Slav peoples of the Ottoman Empire, certainly destined for emancipation, young and heroic races filled with military ardor and needing only leadership, will group themselves around the great Muscovite aggregation which already comprises so many diverse elements. . . .

Distrust, therefore, the ethnography; or rather, do not apply it too strongly to the realm of politics. Under the pretext of a German etymology, Prussia annexes the villages of Lorraine. But what will you say if one day the Slavs should come and vindicate Prussia proper: Pomerania, Silesia, Berlin, because their names are Slavic; if they will do on the banks of the Elbe and Oder what you are doing on the banks of the Moselle; when they will point out, on the map, villages which once were inhabited by Slavic tribes? A nation is not synonymous with race. . . . Britain, which is the most early perfect of all nations, is the most greatly mixed one from the point of view of ethnography and history. . . . Everyone should beware of what is too excessive or too absolute in his mind. . . . Your German race always has the inclination to believe in Valhalla, but Valhalla will never be the Kingdom of God. With her military splendor, Germany risks losing her true vocation. Let all of us together take up the great and true problems, the social problems, which can be summed up in the following manner: to find a rational organization of mankind which would be as just as is humanly possible.

Ernest Renan:
European Peace*

At the beginning of the Franco-Prussian war in the summer of 1870, Renan wrote an article, "The War Between France and Germany," which appeared in the Revue des Deux Mondes *on September 15, 1870. In this article he foresaw some of the worst consequences for Europe and Russia, consequences which have since come true.*

I always regarded the war between France and Germany as the greatest misfortune which could happen to the cause of civilization. . . . In fact, if we leave aside the United States of America, whose undoubtedly brilliant future is still obscure and which in any case occupies a secondary rank in the original labor of the human mind, the intellectual and moral greatness of Europe rests on the Triple Alliance of France, Germany and England. Its rupture would be deeply grievous for progress. United, these three great forces would lead the world and lead it well. They would necessarily lead the other elements, each of considerable importance, which compose Europe. They would, above all, imperiously trace a road for another force which one should neither exaggerate nor depreciate—Russia. Russia is a danger only if the rest of Europe abandons her to the false idea of an originality which she perhaps does not possess, and allows her to unite the barbaric peoples of central Asia. These peoples are entirely powerless by themselves, but they are capable of discipline and unity around a Muscovite Genghis Khan if heed is not taken. The United States can become a danger only if a divided Europe allows it to abandon itself to the lures of a presumptuous youth and to hold resentments against the motherland. . . .

* Ernest Renan, *La Réforme Intellectuelle et Morale* (Cambridge University Press, 1950), pp. 79-104.

The worst consequence of war is to render powerless those who did not desire the war. . . . It opens a fatal circle where common sense is called cowardice and sometimes even treason. Let us speak frankly. One force alone in the world will be able to repair the evil which feudal pride, exaggerated patriotism, the excess of personal power and the low state of parliamentary government on the continent, has cost to civilization. This force is Europe. Europe has a major interest that neither of the two nations should be too victorious or too vanquished. The disappearance of France from among the great powers would mean the end of the European balance. I dare say that Britain especially would feel the conditions of her existence completely changed when such an event should happen. France is one of the conditions of Britain's prosperity. The alliance of France and Britain is well-established for centuries to come. Let Britain think of the United States, of Constantinople, of India; she will always find that she needs France and a strong France. . . .

How could such a horrifying event occur which will leave a memory of terror connected with the year 1870? Because the various European nations are too independent from each other and have no authority above them. There exists neither a congress nor a parliament which would be superior to national sovereignties. Though especially since 1814, Europe has acted frankly as a collective force, the central power has not been strong enough to prevent terrible wars. It must become so strong. That dream of pacifist utopians, a code of justice without an army to uphold its decisions, is a chimera. Nobody will obey it. On the other hand, the opinion that peace can be assured when one nation would have an uncontested superiority over the others is the opposite of the truth; each nation which exercises hegemony prepares its own ruin by this fact alone, because it brings about a coalition of all the other countries against itself. Peace cannot be established and maintained except by the common interest of Europe, or, if one prefers it, by a league of neutral powers ready to enforce peace. Justice has no chance to triumph between two contending parties, but between ten contending parties, justice wins out; for she alone offers a common basis of agreement. The only force capable of upholding a decision for the welfare of the European family against its most powerful member state lies in the power of the various states to unite, to intervene and to mediate. Let us hope that this force will assume ever more concrete and regular forms and will lead in the future to a real congress, meeting periodically if not permanently. It will become the heart of the United States of Europe, bound by a federal pact. . . .

Heinrich von Treitschke:
The Nature of Politics*

Among Treitschke's lecture courses none was as popular as his course on politics. It was the favored course of Treitschke himself, as well as of his students. None of his courses he gave as often as this one. From 1874 on, he repeated it every year. Only after his death in 1897 were the lectures published, in two volumes, mostly from the stenographic notes of some of his students. They appeared in an English translation in 1916 with an introduction by the English statesman Arthur James Balfour, in which the latter wrote that Treitschke's "utopia appears to be a world in which all small Staets had been destroyed, and in which the large States are all either fighting, or preparing for battle."

The entire development of European polity tends unmistakably to drive the second-rate Powers into the background, and this raises issues of immeasurable gravity for the German nation, in the world outside Europe. Up to the present Germany has always had too small a share of the spoils in the partition of non-European territories among the Powers of Europe, and yet our existence as a State of the first rank is vitally affected by the question whether we can become a power beyond the seas. If not, there remains the appalling prospect of England and Russia dividing the world between them, and in such a case it is hard to say whether the Russian knout or the English money bags would be the worst alternative. . . .

When we examine more closely the whole fabric of these conditions of mutual interdependence which we call society we find that under all its forms it tends naturally towards aristocracy.

* Heinrich von Treitschke, *Politics,* English trans. by Mrs. Blanche Dugdale (London: Constable, 1916).

The Social Democrats imply in their very title the absurdity of their aspirations. Just as the State presupposes an irremovable distinction between those in whom authority is vested and those who must submit to it, so also does the nature of society imply differences of social standing and economic condition amongst its members. In short, all social life is built upon class organization. Wise legislation may prevent it from being oppressive and make the transition from class to class as easy as possible, but no power on earth will ever be able to substitute a new and artificial organization of society for the distinctions between its groups which have arisen naturally and automatically.

It is a fundamental rule of human nature that the largest portion of the energy of the human race must be consumed in supplying the primary necessities of existence. The chief aim of a savage's life is to make that life secure, and mankind is by nature so frail and needy that the immense majority of men, even on the higher levels of culture must always and everywhere devote themselves to breadwinning and the material cares of life. To put it simply: the masses must for ever remain the masses. There would be no culture without kitchen-maids.

Obviously education could never thrive if there was nobody to do the rough work. Millions must plough and forge and dig in order that a few thousands may write and paint and study.

It sounds harsh, but it is true for all time, and whining and complaining can never alter it. Moreover the outcry against it does not spring from love of humanity but from the materialism and modern conceit of education. It is profoundly untrue to regard education as the essential factor in history, or as the rock on which human happiness is founded. . . .

Let us hear no clap-trap about the disinherited. No doubt there have been times when those in possession have grossly abused their power, but as a rule the social balance is kept. . . .

The next essential function of the State is the conduct of war. The long oblivion into which this principle had fallen is a proof of how effeminate the science of government had become in civilian hands. In our century this sentimentality was dissipated by Clausewitz, but a one-sided materialism arose in its place, after the fashion of the Manchester school, seeing in man a biped creature, whose destiny lies in buying cheap and selling dear. It is obvious that this idea is not compatible with war, and it is only since the last war [1870-71] that a sounder theory arose of the State and its military power.

Without war no State could be. All those we know of arose through war, and the protection of their members by armed force remains their primary and essential task. War, therefore, will endure to the end of history, as long as there is multiplicity of States. The laws of human thought and of human nature forbid any alternative, neither is one to be wished for. The blind worshipper of an eternal peace falls into the error in isolating the State, or dreams of one which is universal, which we have already seen to be at variance with reason.

Even as it is impossible to conceive of a tribunal above the State, which we have recognized as sovereign in its very essence, so it is likewise impossible to banish the idea of war from the world. It is a favourite fashion of our time to instance England as particularly ready for peace. But England is perpetually at war; there is hardly an instant in her recent history in which she has not been obliged to be fighting somewhere. The great strides which civilization makes against barbarism and unreason are only made actual by the sword. Between civilized nations also war is the form of litigation by which States make their claims valid. The argument brought forward in these terrible lawsuits of the nations compel as no argument in civil suits can ever do. Often as we have tried by theory to convince the small States that Prussia alone can be the leader in Germany, we had to produce the final proof upon the battlefield of Bohemia and the [river] Main [in 1866].

Moreover war is a uniting as well as a dividing element among nations; it does not draw them together in enmity only, for through its means they learn to know and to respect each other's peculiar qualities. . . .

The grandeur of war lies in the utter annihilation of puny man in the great conception of the State, and it brings out the full magnificence of the sacrifice of fellow-countrymen for one another. In war the chaff is winnowed from the wheat. Those who have lived through 1870 cannot fail to understand Niebuhr's description of his feelings in 1813, when he speaks of how no one who has entered into the joy of being bound by a common tie to all his compatriots, gentle and simple alike, can ever forget how he was uplifted by the love, the friendliness, and the strength of that mutual sentiment.

It is war which fosters the political idealism which the materialist rejects. What a disaster for civilization it would be if mankind blotted its heroes from memory. The heroes of a nation are the figures which rejoice and inspire the spirit of its youth, and the writers whose words ring like trumpet blasts become the idols of our boyhood and our early manhood. He who feels no answering thrill is unworthy to bear arms for his country. To appeal from this judgment to Christianity would be sheer perversity, for does not the Bible distinctly say that the ruler shall rule by the sword, and again that greater love no man has than to lay down his life for his friend? To Aryan races, who are before all things courageous, the foolish preaching of everlasting peace has always been vain. They have always been men enough to maintain with the sword what they have attained through the spirit. . . .

The individual should feel himself a member of his State, and as such have courage to take its errors upon him. There must be no question of subjects having the right to oppose a sovereignty which in their opinion is not moral. Cases may arise when the State's action touches the foundation of the moral life, namely, religious feeling. When the Huguenots in France had their religion proscribed and were commanded to worship their God under forms which their deepest conviction held to be unchristian, conscience drove them out from their fatherland, but we must not praise the fine temper of these martyrs for religion from the standpoint of the theologian without recognizing the degree of tragic guilt which is always blended with such moral compulsion. The Huguenots who left their homes were gallant men, no doubt, but each of them had a bitter conflict to fight out within himself before he placed his love for the Heidelberg Catechism above his hereditary love for his country and his king. In modern times there have been Radical parties who have in their vanity imagined themselves faced with a similar struggle, which had in fact only a subjective existence in their own exalted imagination. This was the reason why a number of the German-Americans [after 1848] forsook their fatherland. It is foolish to admire them for this. We must always maintain the principle that the State is in itself an ethical force and a high moral good. . . .

All great nations in the fulness of their strength have desired to set their mark upon barbarian lands. All over the globe today we see the peoples of Europe creating a mighty aristocracy of the white races. Those who take no share in this great rivalry will play a pitiable part in time to come. The colonizing impulse has become a vital question for a great nation. . . .

Fortescue: The Crimean War*

Sir John William Fortescue (1859-1933) was the foremost British military historian. He published his A History of the British Army *in 8 volumes from 1899-1930. In the last volume he discussed aspects of the Crimean War, and wrote about its consequences for Britain.*

In truth the entire episode was far from flattering to us as a nation. Many years later an English Prime Minister declared openly that England in 1854 had followed a false policy in making war upon Russia. She had, as he phrased it, "put her money on the wrong horse." Ministers are not infallible, and indulgence should be extended to their mistakes. But the Crimean War was brought about less through active and consistent decision than through helplessness, improvidence and irresolution, and these are failings which are not so easily forgiven. As to the absurdity of the plan of campaign, the utter ignorance on the part of ministers of the nature and conduct of war, their panic fear of the Press and their consequent disloyalty to their generals, there is no need to say more. Their conduct was most discreditable to them alike as administrators and as the leaders to whom the public at large naturally look for guidance. The Press was undoubtedly more powerful in those days than in these, when the writers for it are so numerous that sheer sense of the ridiculous forbids them to claim infallibility. But a strong minister could, without alienating the Press, still have kept the supreme direction of public opinion in his own hands and inclined it towards calmness and sobriety. A nation, not less surely than a team of horses, instantly detects a weak hand upon the reins and becomes restless and ungovernable.

* From *A History of the British Army,* Vol. XIII, Book XVI, chapter
   XLVII (London: Macmillan and Co., Limited, London, 1930),
   pp. 228-233. Footnotes omitted.

The false judgement of the ministry upon the whole situation was speedily revealed after the first clash of arms. The poor flow of recruits showed plainly enough that the nation's heart was not in the war. There was much foolish hysteria among the public during the South African War of 1899-1902, and there were many childish manifestations in London which it is difficult to recall without shame. Still, when matters went wrong, recruits did at least turn out in tens of thousands and set them right. It was not so in the years of the Crimean War. After the stirring news of Inkerman the monthly influx of recruits was for three months doubled in volume, after which it rapidly subsided. There was no national interest in the struggle; and ministers actually resorted to the condemned methods of the eighteenth century, the levying of mercenaries, to do the work which Englishmen should have done for themselves. Happily none of these ever went into action, and many of the Germans were turned to good account by the grant of lands to them in South Africa, where they made excellent colonists. But the bare fact that they were enlisted at all is a reproach, if not a disgrace.

From a purely military standpoint, the division of supreme command makes it extremely difficult to pass any judgement upon the operations. A difficulty which even Marlborough could not wholly overcome may well have been too great for lesser men. But, passing from the supreme to the subordinate commands, it does not appear that officers had learned many useful lessons from their previous campaigns in India or at the Cape. The circumstances were of course widely different, but Pennefather, who had served under Charles Napier in Sind, and Eyre, who had done well under Harry Smith in South Africa, showed no great intelligence, though boundless courage, before Sevastopol. Nor do the officers in command of battalions, as a rule, appear to have risen to the occasion. The engineers made constant and just complaint of the apathy and carelessness of the regimental officers in charge of working parties; and this would not have occurred had the commanding officers been imbued with the right spirit. It has always been difficult to induce the British soldier to dig, though he will do it for the right officers. On the whole, the campaign was profitable, perhaps, chiefly to intelligent young subalterns who, like Arthur Wellesley in Flanders in 1794, learned much of the way in which things should not be done. Two of these, Garnet Wolseley, the young acting-engineer of the Ninetieth, and Evelyn Wood, the midshipman, brought back from Sebastopol wounds from which they suffered to the end of their days, but lived to do great and lasting good work for the Army.

For the rest the Crimea is interesting as the last appearance of the old long-service soldier in the face of an European enemy. Never did he show himself greater than on the field of Inkerman, when he stood up for hours against odds of five to one, or on the bleak plateau above Sevastopol when he withstood cold and famine until death struck him off the roll of duty, patient and uncomplaining to the last. In any serious war it is always the fate of the existing British army to be destroyed within three months, but none has perished more tragically than this. The long-service soldier was by repute almost outside the pale of civilised society. So little was his real character known that it was a surprise to Miss Nightingale and her nurses to discover that, after all, he was a kindly creature, quickly responsive to gentle handling. The British nation had for generations treated him as an outcast, and done its utmost to make him all that they considered him to be. Yet they despised him chiefly because he was a disciplined man. The discipline of that day was certainly stern; and yet soldiers brought up under that discipline were the model for the constabulary of the whole empire. Nevertheless, through sheer ignorance the public of that day preferred the navvy, who was quite as rough and quite as drunken, simply because he had not, to his great misfortune, been taught to obey.

We have yet to follow the long-service soldier through a few campaigns before he disappears, but the passing bell for him and for much more in the British Army began to sound in the Crimean War. This campaign taught the nation the urgent need for parting with the ways and the traditions that had governed the army with little essential change for two hundred years; and so far it did great good. Yet it is remembered, perhaps, chiefly for three things. The first is that for the first time in the history of war the surgeon's knife was disarmed of half of its terrors by the use of the anæsthetic, chloroform. The second is that reform of hospitals and of the nursing system, already mentioned, which is eternally associated with the name of Florence Nightingale. This was a great work, and has given rise to the legend that all nurses are angels, which is as true or as false as that all soldiers are heroes.

The third is the institution by Queen Victoria of the Victoria Cross. Medals were becoming so common that they had ceased to be distinctive. Even the Order of the Bath had been scattered so widely as to fall into disesteem; so that there was room for a decoration which should really mean that a man had outdone his fellows in daring service. Nevertheless the older officers did not smile upon it. They remembered the days when Englishmen were content to do their duty without hope of outward adornment to their garments; and they recalled with pride Talleyrand's comment when Castlereagh alone of the plenipotentiaries at a congress of all Europe had appeared in a coat unsullied by cordon, star or badge—*Ma foi! c'est tres distingué.* A red ribbon for a few of the most eminent and a blue ribbon for the very highest were the utmost to which any aspired. Charles Stuart took the offer of the knighthood of the Bath as an insult and could hardly be persuaded to accept it. Wellington wished to throw it off when he received the Garter, on the ground that the Sovereign alone could belong to more than one Order. Still, Queen Victoria persevered with impatient eagerness, as her letters show, in the establishment of her new decoration, and the first distribution of it took place on the 26th of June 1857. The material, bronze, was wisely chosen as being of no intrinsic value, and the design was very simple—a Maltese cross, with the Royal crest superimposed, hung from a bar by a link shaped as the letter "V," with the inscription, "For Valour." Old officers continued to sneer at it, telling how men in the ranks, when directed to select one of their comrades for the honour of the Victoria Cross, by no means made valour the ground for their choice. Nor is there the slightest doubt that they spoke the truth. It is, however, long since the Victoria Cross was thus misbestowed. Many a man has earned it who for want of witnesses has never received it; and men have received it in one campaign for deeds that would have passed unnoticed in another and greater. Such accidents are inevitable; but none the less a man who wears the Victoria Cross is now justly sure of the respect and admiration of his fellows; and the decoration is perhaps the most coveted in the world.

Chernyshevsky:
No More Superflous People*

Nikolai Cheryshevsky (1828-1889) was recognized by Russian radical youth as its leader in the 1960's. While imprisoned in St. Petersburg from 1862 to 1864 he wrote a rather artless didactic novel What to Do? *There he told of "the new people" growing up in Russia in full contrast to the "Superfluous," inactive generations preceding them, pictured above all in the novel* Oblomov *(1857) by Ivan Goncharov (1812-1891).*

No More Superfluous People

"One may be gay or not, according to circumstances," said Mr. Beaumont, an American of Russian descent, to his Russian hosts, "but to suffer from ennui is, in my opinion, unpardonable. Ennui is a fashion among our English cousins, but we Americans know nothing about it. We have no time for it, we are too busy. It seems to me that the same should be true of the Russian people also. In my opinion, we have too much to do. But I notice in the Russians just the opposite: they are strongly disposed to spleen. Even the English are not to be compared with them in this respect. English society, looked upon by all Europe as the most tiresome in the world, is more talkative, lively, and gay than Russian society. Russian travelers talk of English spleen; I do not know where their eyes are when they are in their own country."

"But the Russians have good reasons to feel ennui," said Katerina, the host's daughter. "What can they busy themselves about? They have nothing to do. They must sit with folded arms. Name me one occupation, and my ennui probably will vanish."

"You wish to find an occupation? Oh! That is not so difficult:

* From Hans Kohn, *The Mind of Modern Russia* (New York, Harper Torchbooks, 1962).

you see around you such ignorance! Pardon me for speaking to you in this way of your country, but I was born here myself and grew up here, and I consider it as my own, and so I do not stand on ceremony. You see here in Russia an ignorance like that in Turkey or Japan. I hate your native country, since I love it as my own country—may I say, in imitation of your poet. Why, there are so many things here to be done."

"Yes, but what can one man do, to say nothing of one woman?"

"Why, you are doing something already, Katia," said her father. "I will unveil her secret to you, Karl Yakovlich. To drive away ennui she teaches little girls. Every day she receives such pupils, and she devotes three hours to them and sometimes even more."

Beaumont looked at the young girl with esteem: "That is American. By America I mean only the free States of the North. The Southern States are worse than all possible Mexicos, are almost as abominable as Brazil. (As you see, Beaumont was a fervent abolitionist.) It is like us Americans to teach children, but then why do you suffer from ennui?"

"Do you consider that a serious occupation, Mr. Beaumont? It is but a distraction; at least, so it seems to me. Perhaps I am mistaken, and you will call me materialistic."

"Do you expect such a reproach from a man belonging to a nation which everybody reproaches with having no other thought, no other ideal, than dollars?"

"You jest, but I am seriously afraid. I fear to state an opinion on this subject before you. My views might seem to you like those preached by the obscurantists concerning the uselessness of instruction."

"I am an obscurantist myself," replied Beaumont. "I am for the unlettered blacks against their civilized owners in the Southern States. But pardon me, my American hatred has diverted me. It would be very agreeable to me to hear your opinion."

"It is very prosaic, Mr. Beaumont, but I have been led to it by life. It seems to me that the matter with which I occupy myself is but one side of the whole and, moreover, not the side upon which the attention of those who wish to serve the people should be first fixed. This is what I think: give people bread, and they will learn to read themselves. It is necessary to begin with the bread. Otherwise, the time will be wasted."

"Then why don't you begin with the necessary?" said Beaumont. "It is possible. I know examples, with us in America."

"I have already told you why. What can I do alone? I do not know how to go to work; and, even if I knew, could I do it? A young girl is so hampered in every direction. I am free in my own room. But what can I do there? Put a book on the table and teach people to read it. Where can I go? What can I do alone?"

"Are you trying to make me out a despot, Katia?" said her father.

"I blush at the thought, Papa. No, you are good, you do not thwart me. It is society that thwarts me. Is it true, Mr. Beaumont, that in America a young girl is much less hampered?"

"Yes, we may be proud of it, although we are far from where we ought to be. But what a comparison with Europeans! All that you hear about the liberty of women in our country is really the truth."

"Papa, let us go to America, after Mr. Beaumont has bought the factory," said Katerina jokingly. "There I will do something. Ah! How happy I should be!"

"One may find an occupation in St. Petersburg also," said Beaumont.

"How?"

Beaumont hesitated two or three seconds. "But why, then, did I come here? And who could better inform me?" said he to himself. And then he continued, turning to Katia: "Have you not heard of it? There is an attempt in progress here to apply the principles lately deduced by economic science. Are you familiar with them?"

"Yes, I have read a little about that. It must be very interesting and very useful. And could I take part in it? Where shall I find it?"

"In the cooperative shop founded by Madame Kirsonov."

"Is she the doctor's wife?"

"You know him? And has he said nothing to you about this matter?"

"I met him a long time ago. Then he was not yet married. I was sick, and he came several times to treat me and saved my life. Ah! What a man! Does she resemble him?"

Garibaldi: The Sicilian Campaign*

In his autobiography Giuseppe Garibaldi dealt in chapter one of the Third Period with the expedition of the One Thousand Red Shirts to Sicily in May 1860. His autobiography is presented here also for the insight into Garibaldi's passionate personality and romantic style.

Sicily! a filial and well-merited affection makes me consecrate these first words of a glorious period to thee, the land of marvels and of marvellous men. The mother of Archimedes, thy glorious history bears the impress of two achievements paralleled in that of no other nation on earth, however great—two achievements of valour and genius, the first of which proves that there is no tyranny, however firmly constituted, which may not be over-thrown in the dust, crushed into nothingness by the dash, the heroism, of a people like thine, intolerant of outrages. This is the impression left by the sublime, the immortal Vespers. The second belongs to the genius of two boys, who have made it possible to believe in the discoveries of the human mind in the boundless regions of infinity.[1]

Once more, Sicily, it was thine to awaken sleepers, to drag them from the lethargy in which the stupefying poison of diplo-matists and doctrinaires had sunk them—slumberers who, clad in armour not their own, confided to others the safety of their country, thus keeping her dependent and degraded.

Austria is powerful, her armies are numerous; several formi-dable neighbors are opposed, on account of petty dynastic aims, to the resurrection of Italy. The Bourbon has a hundred thousand

---

* *Autobiography* of G. Garibaldi, tr. by A. Werner, Vol. II (London: Walker Smith and Innes, 1889), pp. 143-152.

[1] Two Sicilian boys, not over fourteen years of age, recently succeeded in mentally extracting the algebraic root of the thirty-second power, in the course of a few minutes—a truly stupendous op-eration.

soldiers. Yet what matter? The heart of twenty-five millions throbs and trembles with the love of their country! Sicily, coming forward as champion and representative of these millions, impatient of servitude, has thrown down the gauntlet to tyranny, and defies it everywhere, combating it alike within convent walls and on the peaks of her ever-active volcanoes. But her heroes are few, while the ranks of the tyrant are numerous; and the patriots are scattered, driven from the capital, and forced to take to the mountains. But are not the mountains the refuge, the sanctuary, of the liberty of nations? The Americans, the Swiss, the Greeks, held the mountains when overpowered by the ordered cohorts of their oppressors. "Liberty never escapes those who truly desire to win her." Well has this been proved true by those resolute islanders, who, driven from the cities, kept up the sacred fire in the mountains. Weariness, hardships, sacrifices—what do they matter, when men are fighting for the sacred cause of their country, of humanity?

O noble Thousand! in these days of shame and misery, I love to remember you! Turning to you, the mind feels itself rise above this mephitic atmosphere of robbery and intrigue, relieved to remember that, though the majority of your gallant band have scattered their bones over the battle-fields of liberty, there yet remain enough to represent you, ever ready to prove to your insolent detractors that all are not traitors and cowards—all are not shameless self-seekers, in this land of tyrants and slaves! "Where any of our brothers are fighting for liberty, thither all Italians must hasten!"—such was your motto, and you hastened to the spot without asking whether your foes were few or many, whether the number of true men was sufficient, whether you had the means for the arduous enterprise. You hastened, defying the elements, despising difficulties and dangers and the obstacles thrown in your way by enemies and self-styled friends. In vain did the numerous cruisers of the Bourbon armament surround as with a circle of iron the island about to shake off their yoke; in vain they ploughed the Tyrrhene seas in all directions, to overwhelm you in their abysses—in vain! Sail on, sail on, argonauts of Liberty! There on the utmost verge of the southern horizon shines a star, which will never suffer you to lose your way— which will lead you in safety to the achievement of your quest.

The star seen of the mighty singer of Beatrice—seen of the great ones who came after him, in the darkest hour of the tempest—the Star of Italy! Where are the boats which received you at Villa Spinola, and carried you across the Tyrrhene Sea into the small port of Marsala? Where? Have they been jealously preserved, marked out for the admiration of foreigners and of posterity, as the symbol of the greatest and most honourable enterprise ever undertaken in Italy? Not at all; they have disappeared. Envy and contemptible littleness of mind on the part of Italy's rulers produced a wish to destroy these witnesses to their shame. Some say they perished in a purposely contrived shipwreck. Others suppose them to be rotting in the recesses of some arsenal, Others, again, assert that they have been sold, like worn-out clothes, to the Jews.

Yet sail on, sail on fearlessly, *Piemonte* and *Lombardo,*[2] noble vessels manned by the noblest of crews; history will remember your illustrious names in despite of calumny. And when the survivors of the Thousand, the last spared by the scythe of time, sitting by their own fireside, shall tell their grandchildren of the expedition—mythical as it will seem in those days—in which they were found worthy to share, they will recall to the astonished youth the glorious names of the vessels which composed it.

Sail on! sail on! Ye bear the Thousand, who in later days will become a million—in the day when the blindfolded masses shall understand that the priest is an impostor, and tyrannies a monster anachronism. How glorious were thy Thousand, O Italy, fighting against the plumed and gilded agents of despotism, and driving them before them like sheep!—glorious in their motley array, just as they came from their offices and workshops, at the trumpet-call of duty—in the student's coat and hat, or the more modest garb of the mason, the carpenter, or the smith.[3]

I was in Caprera when I received the first news of a move-

[2] The two steamers which carried the Thousand to Marsala.
[3] From my heart I wish I could have added "of the peasant," but I will not distort the truth. This stalwart and laborious class belongs to the priests, who make it their business to keep it in ignorance. I do not know a single instance of one of its members being seen among the volunteers. They serve in the army, but only when forced to do so; and form the most effectual tools of despotism and priestcraft.

ment at Palermo. Sometimes the talk was of an insurrection which was being propagated, sometimes it was said that the first outbreak had been suppressed. Rumours, however, continued to reach us, of a revolution which, whether suppressed or not, had certainly taken place. I had notice of what had occurred from my friends on the continent. I was asked for the arms and the funds of the "Million of rifles"—the name which had been given to a subscription for the purchase of arms.

Rosalino Pilo and Corrao were preparing to start for Sicily. Knowing the character of those in whose hands was the destiny of Northern Italy, I had not yet shaken off the scepticism into which I had been hurried by the events of the last few months of 1859, and advised them not to act unless we received more positive news about the insurrection. Like the middle-aged man I was, I threw cold water on the strong and ardent resolutions of youthful will. But it was written in the book of destiny that cold water, dogmatism and pedantry should be powerless to obstruct the triumphant march of Italy's fortunes. Though I counselled inaction, action was going on, and the news at last reached us that the Sicilian insurrection was not quelled. I counselled inaction, it is true; but should not the Italian be found wherever the struggle of the national cause against tyranny is going on?

I left Caprera for Genoa, and had some talk on Sicilian affairs with my friends Augier and Coltelletti. Then, at Villa Spinola, in the house of my friend Augusto Vecchi, we began to make arrangements for an expedition.

Bixio was certainly the prime mover in this astonishing enterprise. His courage, activity, and experience of the sea, especially in the neighbourhood of Genoa, his native place were of enormous value in facilitating our proceedings.

Crispi, La Masa, Orsini, Calvino, Castiglia, the Orlandi, Carini, and others, were the most enthusiastic for the expedition among the Sicilians, and also Stocco and Plutino of Calabria. All were agreed that, whatever happened, if the Sicilians were fighting, we must go, whether there was any probability of success or not.

However, a few discouraging rumours came very near putting an end to the whole thing. A telegram from Malta, sent by a trustworthy friend, announced that all was lost, and that the survivors of the Sicilian revolution had taken refuge in that island.

We were near desisting from the enterprise, though I ought to acknowledge that the faith of the above-mentioned Sicilians never failed, and that they were still determined to try their luck under the guidance of the gallant Bixio, and at least to ascertain, on Sicilian ground, how matters stood.

Meanwhile Cavour's Government was beginning that system of petty intrigue and contemptible opposition, which pursued our expedition to the last. Cavour's followers could not have said, "We do not want an expedition into Sicily;" public opinion would have declared them reprobates, and that fictitious popularity, gained by the wholesale purchase (with the nation's money) of men and newspapers, would probably have been shaken.

I could therefore prepare some help for our friends fighting in Sicily, with little fear of being arrested by these gentlemen, and with the support of the people's generous feelings, deeply stirred as they were by the manly resolution of the brave islanders. Only despair, and the iron resolution of the men of the Vespers, could push forward such an insurrection. La Farina, deputed by Cavour to watch our movements, showed his want of faith in the enterprise, and made use, in order to dissuade me from it, of his knowledge of the Sicilian people, being himself a native of the island. He alleged that the insurgents, having lost Palermo, were hopelessly ruined. However, a Government notice which he himself gave us, helped to strengthen us in our resolve of immediate action. At Milan we had some 15,000 good rifles, in addition to the pecuniary means at our disposal. At the head of the management of the "Million rifles" fund were Besana and Finzi, both trustworthy men. I sent for Besana, who arrived at Genoa with a sum of money, leaving orders for rifles, ammunition, and other necessaries of war, to be sent to us from Milan. At the same time Bixio was in treaty with Fauché, of the Rubattino Steamship Company, for our passage to Sicily. The affair went off all right, and, thanks to the activity of Fauché and Bixio, and the noble impetuosity of the Italian youth, who hastened from all sides to join us, we found ourselves, in a few days, quite ready to take the sea, when an unexpected incident not only retarded our enterprise, but almost rendered it impossible.

The men sent by me to receive the rifles at Milan found at the doors of the depôt the royal carbineers, who intimated to them that they were not to take away a single rifle. This order had been given by Cavour.

This obstacle, though it did not fail to thwart and annoy us, could not make us desist from our project; and, as we could not have our own arms, we attempted to get others elsewhere. We should certainly have procured them in one way or another, when La Farina offered a thousand rifles and eight thousand francs, which I, unwilling to bear malice, accepted.

It was a cunning act of liberality on the part of those highly placed foxes, since in reality we were deprived of the good guns which had remained at Milan, and found ourselves forced to use the very inferior article procured by La Farina.

My comrades of Calatafimi can describe the wretched arms with which they had to meet the good Bourbon carbines in that glorious conflict. All this delayed our departure, so that we were obliged to send home many volunteers, their numbers becoming too great for an insufficient means of transport, and because we had no wish uselessly to arouse the suspicions of the police— the French and Sardinian not excepted. The firm determination to do something, and not desert our Sicilian friends, at last over- came every obstacle. The volunteers who had been destined for the expedition were recalled, and came at once—especially from Lombardy. The Genoese had remained in readiness all the time. The arms, ammunition, provisions, and a small quantity of bag- gage, were embarked on board some little boats. Two steamers, the *Lombardo* and the *Piemonte,* the former commanded by Bixio, and the latter by Castiglia, were fixed on; and on the night of May 5 we left the harbour of Genoa, in order to take on board the men who were awaiting us, divided between La Foce and Villa Spinola.

We did not fail to meet with some difficulties, inseparable from an enterprise of this kind.

To board the two steamers at anchor in the harbour at Genoa, just under the Darsena, to overpower the crew and force them to assist us, then to get up steam and take the *Lombardo* in tow of the *Piemonte,* and all this by moonlight—these are actions easier to describe than to perform, and needing great coolness, skill, and good fortune to execute them successfully. The two Sicilians, Orlando and Campo, who formed part of the expedition, and were both engineers, were of the greatest use to us on this occasion.

By dawn all were on board. The joy of danger and adventure, and the consciousness of serving their country's sacred cause, were stamped on the countenances of the Thousand. There were a thousand of them, nearly all Alpine *cacciatori*—those same men whom Cavour, a few months ago, had abandoned in the heart of Lombardy during the Austrian war, and to whom he had refused to send the reinforcements ordered by the King. They were those same Alpine *cacciatori* who were received by the ministry at Turin—being, unhappily, compelled to apply to the latter—as if infected with the plague, and as such driven away; the same Thousand who twice presented themselves at Genoa to run a positive risk, and who always will present themselves wherever there is a chance of giving their lives for Italy, asking for no other reward than the approval of their consciences.

They were glorious, my young veterans of Italian liberty; and I, proud of their faith in me, felt capable of attempting anything.

Marx: Critique of Political Economy*

Marx published in 1859 his A Contribution to the Critique of Political Economy. *It was the year of H. J. S. Mill's* On Liberty *and Darwin's* On the Origin of Species. *The Preface to Marx's book, which is reprinted here, gives a clear résumé of the development of his thought and of his theory of history.*

I consider the system of bourgeois economy in the following order: *Capital, landed property, wage labor; state, foreign trade, world market.* Under the first three heads I examine the conditions of the economic existence of the three great classes, which make up modern bourgeois society; the connection of the three remaining heads is self evident. The first part of the first book, treating of capital, consists of the following chapters: 1. Commodity; 2. Money, or simple circulation; 3. Capital in general. The first two chapters form the contents of the present work. The entire material lies before me in the form of monographs, written at long intervals not for publication, but for the purpose of clearing up those questions to myself, and their systematic elaboration on the plan outlined above will depend upon circumstances.

I omit a general introduction which I had prepared, as on second thought any anticipation of results that are still to be proven, seemed to me objectionable, and the reader who wishes to follow me at all, must make up his mind to pass from the special to the general. On the other hand, some remarks as to the course of my own politico-economic studies may be in place here.

The subject of my professional studies was jurisprudence, which I pursued, however, in connection with and as secondary to the studies of philosophy and history. In 1842-43, as editor of

---

* From Karl Marx, *A Contribution to the Critique of Political Economy,* tr. from the second German edition by N. J. Stone (Chicago: Charles H. Kerr & Company, 1904), pp. 9-15.

the "Rheinische Zeitung," I found myself embarrassed at first when I had to take part in discussions concerning so-called material interests. The proceedings of the Rhine Diet in connection with forest thefts and the extreme subdivision of landed property; the official controversy about the condition of the Mosel peasants into which Herr von Schaper, at that time president of the Rhine Province, entered with the "Rheinische Zeitung;" finally, the debates on free trade and protection, gave me the first impulse to take up the study of economic questions. At the same time a weak, quasi-philosophic echo of French socialism and communism made itself heard in the "Rheinische Zeitung" in those days when the good intentions "to go ahead" greatly outweighed knowledge of facts. I declared myself against such botching, but had to admit at once in a controversy with the "Allgemeine Augsburger Zeitung" that my previous studies did not allow me to hazard an independent judgment as to the merits of the French schools. When, therefore, the publishers of the "Rheinische Zeitung" conceived the illusion that by a less aggressive policy the paper could be saved from the death sentence pronounced upon it, I was glad to grasp that opportunity to retire to my study room from public life.

The first work undertaken for the solution of the question that troubled me, was a critical revision of Hegel's "Philosophy of Law"; the introduction to that work appeared in the "Deutsch-Französische Jahrbücher," published in Paris in 1844. I was led by my studies to the conclusion that legal relations as well as forms of state could neither be understood by themselves, nor explained by the so-called general progress of the human mind, but that they are rooted in the material conditions of life, which are summed up by Hegel after the fashion of the English and French of the eighteenth century under the name "civic society;" the anatomy of that civic society is to be sought in political economy. The study of the latter which I had taken up in Paris, I continued at Brussels whither I emigrated on account of an order of expulsion issued by Mr. Guizot. The general conclusion at which I arrived and which, once reached, continued to serve as the leading thread in my studies, may be briefly summed up as follows: 1) In the social production which men carry on they enter into definite relations that are indispensable and independent of their will; these relations of production correspond to a definite stage of development of their material powers of production. 2) The sum total of these relations of production constitutes the economic structure of society—the real foundation, on which rise legal and political superstructures and to which correspond definite forms of social consciousness. 3) The mode of production in material life determines the general character of the social, political and spiritual processes of life. 4) It is not the consciousness of men that determines their existence, but, on the contrary, their social existence determines their consciousness. 5) At a certain stage of their development, the material forces of production in society come in conflict with the existing relations of production, or—what is but a legal expression for the same thing—with the property relations within which they had been at work before. From forms of development of the forces of production these relations turn into their fetters. Then comes the period of social revolution. With the change of the economic foundation the entire immense superstructure is more or less rapidly transformed. In considering such transformations the distinction should always be made between the material transformation of the economic conditions of production which can be determined with the precision of natural science, and the legal, political, religious, aesthetic or philosophic—in short ideological forms in which men become conscious of this conflict and fight it out. Just as our opinion of an individual is not based on what he thinks of himself, so can we not judge of such a period of transformation by its own consciousness; on the contrary, this consciousness must rather be explained from the contradictions of material life, from the existing conflict between the social forces of production and the relations of production. No social order ever disappears before all the productive forces, for which there is room in it, have been developed; and new higher relations of production never appear before the material conditions of their existence have matured in the womb of the old society. Therefore, mankind always takes up only such problems as it can solve; since, looking at the matter more closely, we will always find that the problem itself arises only when the material conditions necessary for its solution already exist or are at least in the process of formation. In broad outlines we can designate the

Asiatic, the ancient, the feudal, and the modern bourgeois methods of production as so many epochs in the progress of the economic formation of society. (The bourgeois relations of production are the last antagonistic form of the social process of production—antagonistic not in the sense of individual antagonism, but of one arising from conditions surrounding the life of individuals in society;) at the same time the productive forces developing in the womb of bourgeois society create the material conditions for the solution of that antagonism. This social formation constitutes, therefore, the closing chapter of the prehistoric stage of human society.

Frederick Engels, with whom I was continually corresponding and exchanging ideas since the appearance of his ingenious critical essay on economic categories (in the "Deutsch-Französische Jahrbücher"), came by a different road to the same conclusions as myself (see his "Condition of the Working Classes in England"). When he, too, settled in Brussels in the spring of 1845, we decided to work out together the contrast between our view and the idealism of the German philosophy, in fact to settle our accounts with our former philosophic conscience. The plan was carried out in the form of a criticism of the post-Hegelian philosophy. The manuscript in two solid octavo volumes had long reached the publisher in Westphalia, when we received information that conditions had so changed as not to allow of its publication. We abandoned the manuscript to the stinging criticism of the mice the more readily since we had accomplished our main purpose—the clearing up of the question to ourselves. Of the scattered writings on various subjects in which we presented our views to the public at that time, I recall only the "Manifesto of the Communist Party" written by Engels and myself, and the "Discourse on Free Trade" written by myself. The leading points of our theory were first presented scientifically, though in a polemic form, in my "Misère de la Philosophie, etc." directed against Proudhon and published in 1847. An essay on "Wage Labor," written by me in German, and in which I put together my lectures on the subject delivered before the German Workmen's Club at Brussels, was prevented from leaving the hands of the printer by the February revolution and my expulsion from Belgium which followed it as a consequence.

The publication of the "Neue Rheinische Zeitung" in 1848 and 1849, and the events which took place later on, interrupted my economic studies which I could not resume before 1850 in London. The enormous material on the history of political economy which is accumulated in the British Museum; the favorable view which London offers for the observation of bourgeois society; finally, the new stage of development upon which the latter seemed to have entered with the discovery of gold in California and Australia, led me to the decision to resume my studies from the very beginning and work up critically the new material. These studies partly led to what might seem side questions, over which I nevertheless had to stop for longer or shorter periods of time. Especially was the time at my disposal cut down by the imperative necessity of working for a living. My work as contributor on the leading Anglo-American newspaper, the "New York Tribune," at which I have now been engaged for eight years, has caused very great interruption in my studies, since I engage in newspaper work proper only occasionally. Yet articles on important economic events in England and on the continent have formed so large a part of my contributions that I have been obliged to make myself familiar with practical details which lie outside the proper sphere of political economy.

This account of the course of my studies in political economy is simply to prove that my views, whatever one may think of them, and no matter how little they agree with the interested prejudices of the ruling classes, are the result of many years of conscientious research. At the entrance to science, however, the same requirement must be put as at the entrance to hell:

> Qui si convien lasciare ogni sospetto
> Ogni viltà convien che qui sia morta.[1]

[1] Here all mistrust must be abandoned and here must perish every craven thought.—ED.

Bibliography of Paperbacks

Barzun, Jacques, *Darwin, Marx, Wagner* (Anchor).

Berlin, Isaiah, *Karl Marx, his Life and Environment* (Oxford U. Press).

Binkley, Robert C., *Realism and Nationalism 1852-1871* (Torchbook Harper).

Briggs, Asa, *Victorian People* (Harper Colophon).

Hales, E. E. Y., *Pio Nono* (Doubleday Image Books).

Kohn, Hans, *Prophets and Peoples. Studies in Nineteenth Century Nationalism* (Collier).

————*Pan-Slavism* (Vintage).

Mosse, W. E., *Alexander II and the Modernization of Russia* (Collier).

Salvadori, Massimo, *Cavour and the Unification of Italy* (Anvil).

Schapiro, J. Salwyn, *Movements of Social Dissent in Modern Europe* (Anvil).

Snyder, Louis, *Basic History of Modern Germany* (Anvil).

Stavrianos, L. S., *The Balkans 1815-1914* (Berkshire Studies in History).

Wallace, Sir Donald MacKenzie, *Russia on the Eve of War and Revolution* (Vintage).

Young, G. M., *Victorian England. Portrait of an Age* (Oxford U. Press).

———— *Victorian Essays* (Oxford U. Press).

Index

189

VAN NOSTRAND ANVIL BOOKS already published